# Realism in Political Theory

Over the past decade, an intellectual movement known as "realism" has challenged the reigning orthodoxy in political theory and political philosophy. Realists take issue with what they see as the excessive moralism and utopianism associated with prominent philosophers like John Rawls, Ronald Dworkin, and G.A. Cohen; but what they would put in its place has not always been clear. The contributors to this volume seek to bring realism into a new phase, constructive rather than merely combative. To this end they examine three distinct kinds of realism. The first seeks to place questions of feasibility at the center of political theory and philosophy; the second seeks to reorient our interpretations of key works in the canon; the third seeks new interpretations or specifications of prominent ideologies such as liberalism, radicalism, and republicanism such that they no longer rely on abstract or systematic philosophic systems. Contributors include: David Estlund, Edward Hall, Alison McQueen, Terry Nardin, Philip Pettit, Janosch Prinz, Enzo Rossi, Andrew Sabl, Rahul Sagar, and Matt Sleat.

The chapters in this book were originally published as a special issue of *Critical Review of International Social and Political Philosophy*.

**Rahul Sagar** is Global Network Associate Professor of Political Science, NYU Abu Dhabi, UAE.

**Andrew Sabl** is Orrick Fellow and Visiting Professor in the Program on Ethics, Politics and Economics, Yale University, USA.

# Realism in Political Theory

*Edited by*
**Rahul Sagar and Andrew Sabl**

LONDON AND NEW YORK

First published 2018 by Routledge

2 Park Square, Milton Park, Abingdon, Oxon OX14 4RN
605 Third Avenue, New York, NY 10017

*Routledge is an imprint of the Taylor & Francis Group, an informa business*

First issued in paperback 2021

Chapters 1–5, 7–8 © 2018 Taylor & Francis
Chapter 6 © 2018 Janosch Prinz and Enzo Rossi. Originally published as Open Access.

All rights reserved. No part of this book may be reprinted or reproduced or utilised in any form or by any electronic, mechanical, or other means, now known or hereafter invented, including photocopying and recording, or in any information storage or retrieval system, without permission in writing from the publishers.

Notice:
Product or corporate names may be trademarks or registered trademarks, and are used only for identification and explanation without intent to infringe.

Publisher's Note

The publisher has gone to great lengths to ensure the quality of this reprint but points out that some imperfections in the original copies may be apparent.

*British Library Cataloguing in Publication Data*
A catalogue record for this book is available from the British Library

ISBN 13: 978-0-8153-4780-4 (hbk)

ISBN 13: 978-0-367-53058-7 (pbk)

Typeset in Myriad Pro
by RefineCatch Limited, Bungay, Suffolk

**Publisher's Note**
The publisher accepts responsibility for any inconsistencies that may have arisen during the conversion of this book from journal articles to book chapters, namely the possible inclusion of journal terminology.

**Disclaimer**
Every effort has been made to contact copyright holders for their permission to reprint material in this book. The publishers would be grateful to hear from any copyright holder who is not here acknowledged and will undertake to rectify any errors or omissions in future editions of this book.

Printed in the United Kingdom
by Henry Ling Limited

# Contents

*Citation Information*   vii
*Notes on Contributors*   ix

1. Introduction   1
   *Andrew Sabl and Rahul Sagar*

2. Ethics, morality and the case for realist political theory   10
   *Edward Hall and Matt Sleat*

3. Political realism and the realist 'Tradition'   28
   *Alison McQueen*

4. The new realism and the old   46
   *Terry Nardin*

5. Political realism meets civic republicanism   63
   *Philip Pettit*

6. Political realism as ideology critique   80
   *Janosch Prinz and Enzo Rossi*

7. Realist liberalism: an agenda   98
   *Andrew Sabl*

8. Methodological moralism in political philosophy   117
   *David Estlund*

*Index*   135

# Citation Information

The chapters in this book were originally published in *Critical Review of International Social and Political Philosophy*, volume 20, issue 3 (2017). When citing this material, please use the original page numbering for each article, as follows:

**Chapter 1**
*Introduction*
Andrew Sabl and Rahul Sagar
*Critical Review of International Social and Political Philosophy*, volume 20, issue 3 (2017), pp. 269–277

**Chapter 2**
*Ethics, morality and the case for realist political theory*
Edward Hall and Matt Sleat
*Critical Review of International Social and Political Philosophy*, volume 20, issue 3 (2017), pp. 278–295

**Chapter 3**
*Political realism and the realist 'Tradition'*
Alison McQueen
*Critical Review of International Social and Political Philosophy*, volume 20, issue 3 (2017), pp. 296–313

**Chapter 4**
*The new realism and the old*
Terry Nardin
*Critical Review of International Social and Political Philosophy*, volume 20, issue 3 (2017), pp. 314–330

**Chapter 5**
*Political realism meets civic republicanism*
Philip Pettit
*Critical Review of International Social and Political Philosophy*, volume 20, issue 3 (2017), pp. 331–347

## Chapter 6
*Political realism as ideology critique*
Janosch Prinz and Enzo Rossi
*Critical Review of International Social and Political Philosophy*, volume 20, issue 3 (2017), pp. 348–365

## Chapter 7
*Realist liberalism: an agenda*
Andrew Sabl
*Critical Review of International Social and Political Philosophy*, volume 20, issue 3 (2017), pp. 366–384

## Chapter 8
*Methodological moralism in political philosophy*
David Estlund
*Critical Review of International Social and Political Philosophy*, volume 20, issue 3 (2017), pp. 385–402

For any permission-related enquiries please visit:
http://www.tandfonline.com/page/help/permissions

# Notes on Contributors

**David Estlund** is Lombardo Family Professor of Humanities and Philosophy at Brown University, USA. He is the author of *Democratic Authority* (Princeton, 2008) and editor of *The Oxford Handbook of Political Philosophy* (Oxford, 2012).

**Edward Hall** is Lecturer in Political Theory at the University of Sheffield, UK. His teaching and research focuses on contemporary political theory, British political thought, and political ethics. He has published articles in journals including: *European Journal of Political Theory*, *Political Studies*, *Social Philosophy and Policy*, and *Social Theory and Practice*.

**Alison McQueen** is Assistant Professor in the Department of Political Science at Stanford University, USA. Her research focuses on religion in early modern political thought, the history of International Relations thought, and methods of textual analysis. Her work has been published or is forthcoming in *Journal of Politics*, *European Journal of Political Theory*, *American Political Thought*, and *Political Theory*.

**Terry Nardin** is Professor of Social Sciences and Director of the Common Curriculum at Yale-NUS College in Singapore. He is the author of *Law, Morality, and the Relations of States* and *The Philosophy of Michael Oakeshott*, and editor or co-editor of several books on political theory. His most recent articles have appeared in *European Journal of International Law*, *Global Discourse*, and *History of European Ideas*.

**Philip Pettit** is L.S. Rockefeller University Professor of Human Values at Princeton, USA, and Distinguished Professor of Philosophy at the ANU.

**Janosch Prinz** is a Leverhulme Early Career Fellow at the University of East Anglia, UK. His main research interest is the nature and value of (realist) political and social theory. His fellowship aims at developing a diagnostic approach to democratic legitimacy. He currently explores the intersection of normative and empirical considerations in the conduct of political inquiry.

**Enzo Rossi** teaches Political Theory at the University of Amsterdam, the Netherlands. He is a co-editor of the *European Journal of Political Theory* and a principal investigator of the Dutch National Science Organisation project "Legitimacy Beyond Consent" (2016–2021). His main current project is a realist critical theory of legitimacy.

**Andrew Sabl** is Orrick Fellow and Visiting Professor (2013–18) in the Program on Ethics, Politics and Economics, Yale University, USA. He is the author of *Ruling Passions: Political Offices and Democratic Ethics* (2002) and *Hume's Politics: Coordination and Crisis in the History of England* (2012).

**Rahul Sagar** is Global Network Associate Professor of Political Science at NYU Abu Dhabi, UAE. He is the author of *Secrets and Leaks: The Dilemma of State Secrecy* (Princeton University Press, 2013).

**Matt Sleat** is a Reader in Political Theory at the University of Sheffield, UK. He is the author of numerous articles on liberal and realist thought and his monograph *Liberal Realism* was published in 2013.

# Introduction

Andrew Sabl and Rahul Sagar

**ABSTRACT**
The realist movement in political thought has until recently been defined as much by its enemies as by its theses. It has often spent more time explaining what was wrong with ideal theory than doing realist theory. This essay argues that realism is entering a new phase, constructive rather than combative. It identifies three modes of constructive or affirmative realist theory (present in this volume's essays and elsewhere). The first focuses on feasibility; the second revisits the realist canon; and the third shows how familiar ideologies can be defended without appealing to the abstract or abstruse philosophical claims on which they are often sought to rely. The essay does not seek unity where none can be found. It counsels accepting that the family surnamed Realism is a large and nontraditional one in which splits and remarriages are not unknown and many prospective partners raise eyebrows.

This collection of essays emerges from a workshop held at the National University of Singapore that focused on identifying where 'Realism' has come from and where it might be headed. William Galston's famous review article, one of the first to christen realism as a definable movement, essentially defined it as a 'dissenting movement' against the ideal theory practiced by Rawls and by many deliberative democrats (2010, 386). The label 'realist' applied to a political theory came to mean, in effect, 'different from ideal theory' in one or more respects. A realist theory might be determined to provide practical advice (as opposed to justifying abstract ideals); concerned with political feasibility (as opposed to making implausible assumptions and demands); interested in rhetoric and persuasion (as opposed to technical philosophical argumentation); or eager to bring in historical and political facts as sources of good political judgment (as opposed to abstracting from real world cases and our intuitions about them).

This essentially negative definition was valuable and by no means inaccurate. Since much early realism amounted to declarations of independence from a form of political theory that realists regarded as hegemonic, it tended to be apologetic and 'meta': realists spent more time explaining what was wrong with 'ideal theory' than they spent doing 'realist theory.' Related to this, early realism was often unclear as to what it was actually aiming at – for instance, whether it aimed at immediate relevance at the risk of excessive deference to current opinion, or whether it sought deep truths about ethics, politics, and society, asking deep questions about the nature of power and its relation to truth, at the risk of abstruseness. Eager to escape the Rawlsian camp, many realists understandably cared more about justifying the exodus, and linking up with other existing or potential refugees, than about which path out they took.

More recently, however, some of the defensiveness has faded. Sabl (2015) has distinguished 'wet' realism, which retains a concern with legitimation and justification, from a 'dry' realism that rejects it. A growing number of realists are quite dry without feeling the need to stress their dryness; they do not so much reject the idealist liberal's demand for justification as simply regard it as irrelevant to their projects. This seems a sign of realism's new-found strength and confidence.

As the number of those who profess some interest in realism has increased, recruitment and morale have become less important than making strong and interesting substantive claims – at the cost, inevitably, of some schisms. The articles in this symposium reflect this trend.[1] In particular, they embody realist theory of three kinds that we are convinced will largely define the field – or rather fields – of study well into the future. We distinguish these three kinds of realism by their temporal dimension: the first is oriented towards the future; the second, towards the past; the third, towards the present.

## The three futures of realism

One kind of realism concerns itself with *feasibility and real-world constraints*. It invites normative theory to undertake a kind of due diligence: that is, to evaluate the plausibility of its assumptions and the feasibility of its prescriptions. This is not to imply that a normative theory should have no 'aspirational' content whatsoever (Estlund 2014). Rather, as Galston writes, this approach seeks to locate 'the outer perimeter of the desirable possible and to use it as a guide for action in the here and now' (2010, 401). In the current collection, this form of realism can be discerned in Pettit's essay. Perhaps characteristically for this kind of realism, his endorsement takes adjectival form: his preferred form of republican thought is realis*tic,* attuned to real-world constraints, as well as 'practical,' able to 'guide people in deciding about the political interventions they ought to pursue in their own society.'

On the other hand, Hall and Sleat's contribution to this model sets itself up in direct *contrast* with a 'non-ideal' or feasibility-based view; those authors distinguish their own preferred form of realism, one devoted to the study of politics as the source of ethical truth, from the kind for which feasibility is a central concern.

A deeper concern with feasibility might, however, render both these declarations, of allegiance and enmity, a bit more problematic. For instance, to the extent that national security requires not just occasional but widespread secrecy (Sagar 2013), we might even question the plausibility of liberal and republican models of politics, both of which require public and transparent deliberation and contestation. Thus, while making a normative theory 'realistic' may seem to involve only common-sense pragmatism, it could in fact force much deeper rethinking. This observation points to a distinction, often not well understood, between realism and non-ideal theory. Whereas the latter explains how to move towards a more ideal world given our present, imperfect circumstances, but does not question the value of the ideal itself, the former can question ideals themselves (Sagar 2011).

By the same token, grappling with questions of feasibility and implementation may require facing deeper, more troubling, and less obvious truths about ethics than those who distinguish non-ideal theory from a Nietzschean attachment to 'truthfulness,' as Hall and Sleat would like to do, might admit. When we battle the recalcitrance of domestic and international politics, we may become a bit recalcitrant, disinclined to gloss politics as harmonic and consensual, ourselves; when we look deeply and unflinchingly into hard realities, they might look back at us.

A second kind of realism might be called *historical or interpretive*. Just as a rejection of ideal theory alerts us to new possibilities regarding the future (as well as suggesting that some that we thought open might in fact be closed), it also alerts us to ways of complicating the 'traditions' we construct regarding the past. The Rawlsian story, as noted by McQueen, puts forth a deliberately stylized narrative in which societies gradually learn the institutional and ethical prerequisites of citizens treating one another as free and equal. One way in which a realist perspective can, and often does, complicate such narratives is by substituting *another* usable or monumental history of ideas, involving a realist counter-canon and, presumably, another story of historical progress. McQueen rejects this program of constructing what might be called an 'edifying' tradition for realism, fit to compete with others that are equally monumental and misleading. Translating from the history of liberalism to that of realism Duncan Bell's distinction between realist arguments and realist thinkers, she proposes ways of including a range of past writers in the history of realism without imagining that they considered themselves realists or that realism exhausts their thought. McQueen comes to praise the right kind of realist tradition, not to bury it: by incorporating a wider range of thinkers while remaining, as it were, realistic about the extent of their affinity with realist theorizing as we now do it, we can both learn unexpected things from the past and draw on past thinkers' resources to strengthen realist arguments in the present.

Less radically, but in a surprisingly similar vein, Nardin's article, which may be considered a friendly amendment to Kantian historiography from a realist direction, is determined to show that the history of liberalism is less uniformly 'ethics-first' and 'idealist' than realists – and, one might add, many liberals – imagine. As Nardin documents, no less than Kant placed at the center of his political theory not the demands of his moral philosophy but those of politics. If an awareness of 'coercive politics' (Stears 2007; similarly Prinz and Rossi in this volume) or 'the autonomy of the political' (Rossi and Sleat 2014) are sometimes considered the hallmarks of realist thinking, then on Nardin's view we must consider Kant a realist. A political association is by definition 'non-voluntary,' and Kantianism is about deliberating the terms on which coercion will take place. At this point, however, Nardin makes the very Kantian claim that 'political discourse must identify the boundaries between legitimate restraint and illegitimate oppression.' A realist might (and Sabl in this volume does) question the status of this 'must' – that is, a realist will question whether discourses of legitimacy seem obviously important to all citizens, or just to those steeped in Kantian philosophy.

To note this, however, is to see in action the fruitful and exciting potential for historical arguments to interact with contemporary ones. To the extent that coercion and the autonomy of politics do not distinguish Kant's thought from that of canonical or current realists, perhaps we must re-evaluate the alleged centrality of coercion and the autonomy of politics to the specifically realist approach. Perhaps what distinguishes realists is not truth-telling regarding politics' means, nor a special ontological appreciation of 'the political,' but a disinclination to regard moral considerations – whether they involve justice or legitimacy – as political theory's central concern. To the extent that realists are determined to retain the autonomy of politics as a central category, they may have to state more clearly what they mean by such autonomy. It cannot merely be that the normative problems and solutions pertaining to politics differ substantially from those pertaining to private life (since Kant thinks that too). It must be more a matter of whether attention to politics can alert us to a range of ethical truths that abstract and politically unaware philosophizing tends to miss (the Hall and Sleat claim, which might be called 'enlightening' mode of connecting politics to truthfulness) or else undermine moral standards that politically unaware philosophizing takes for granted (the Prinz and Rossi claim, which might be called the 'debunking' or 'critical' mode).

This last possibility bears on the third strand of realism represented here, which is *programmatic* in nature – or perhaps 'ideological,' in the benign sense: it strives self-consciously to connect analyses of how things stand to crucial questions regarding what should be done (MacIntyre 1978). This strand aims to rethink, in realist mode, familiar schools of ideological thought. It is commonly observed (though also contested) that realism as such is more or less agnostic: compatible with many ideological positions. The flip side of this is that almost every ideological position can be fruitfully re-examined, and possibly rebuilt, if we ask what it would look like with its idealist scaffolding removed and a realist renovation put in its place.

Pettit's contribution provides an ideal example because it presents republicanism without relying significantly on philosophical arguments in defense of the claim that liberty should be regarded primarily as non-domination. While Pettit in other work certainly endorses that claim, and has supplied the grounding for it, his work here is striking for its ability to vindicate republicanism without it. Here (as in other recent work that he cites), Pettit rests republican institutions and practices primarily on the felt aspirations and the palpable, overt political worries of actual citizens. Without calling for the rejection of the systematic philosophizing that republicanism has often been thought to require, his article invites the conclusion that we could probably do so if we wished. Republicanism, in this framing, is not 'a philosopher's invention' so much as 'an articulation of a concern that all of us have in our dealings with others.'

Similarly, Prinz and Rossi's contribution here might be summarized as 'critical theory without ideal speech.' They propose a form of *Ideologiekritik* that is 'internal to the political context without being internal to the ideology that underpins that context.' This critique, which presses on political judgments in order to defamiliarize them and expose their groundings in social power, in no way requires Habermasian ideals or rationalist standards. (To the extent that Prinz and Rossi draw on philosophy, it is not standard moral philosophy, in either continental or Anglo-American form, but philosophy of language.)

Finally, Sabl offers an account of 'realist liberalism.' He denies that liberalism depends on achieving 'normative consensus' (since modern societies are unlikely to attain such a consensus); that it requires 'regulative ideals' (since visions that animate political forces do not derive from rigorous, systematic philosophy); and that its policies must 'be justified' (since such policies have, in practice, been enforced without regard for whether opponents might 'reasonably reject' them). In reality, Sabl claims, key liberal institutions – such as free speech, toleration, markets, and the welfare state – emerge or evolve because they further common interests and help to settle clashes among conflicting interests. Because they serve 'multiple and indefinite purposes,' and because they are not the product of 'a deliberate plan,' such institutions, Sabl warns, will come into conflict with each other. Yet because they derive their persistent popularity and de facto authority from their utility (in the Humean sense: widespread advantageousness) rather than from systematic normative foundations, they can 'lumber on adequately well.'

## Ethics beyond regulatory ideals

David Estlund's contribution to this volume has so far gone largely unmentioned. Estlund, while himself no realist, does realism a profound service by reading the realist literature with care and respect while insisting that it make its central claims quite a bit clearer. He calls on realists to specify precisely what they mean by rejecting which kind of moral standards (as well as how their allegedly non-moralist normativity will be able to avoid the charges realists level at the moralist kind), and what they intend in claiming that 'politics' can do without moral evaluation. We will not try here to summarize his characteristically careful and thorough argument. But we would like to pursue the implications of his final metaphor, which compares realists who 'reject' the idea of evaluating political arrangements by moral standards to those who ignore bad medical news:

> If one doctor tells me I have leukemia, and I seek a second opinion, I want another opinion about whether I have leukemia, not about how acute my eye-sight is, or about how well I tend my garden. There might be good things about my health, or other aspects of my life, but they change the subject. They are irrelevant to the initial troubling diagnosis. Similarly, to "reject" the whole moralized framework of social justice and injustice, as many authors do, is one thing. To cast any serious doubt on it is another.

Let us push on this a bit.

First: to the extent that Hall and Sleat (and in a different way, Prinz and Rossi) are right to see realism as aspiring to normative or evaluative – though perhaps not narrowly 'moral' – truths that standard moral theory cannot grasp, they are calling not for ignoring medical advice but for seeking a fuller, wiser, kind of medicine. Perhaps realists are like osteopaths, who see that a moralistic pill cannot cure society's ills because the problem goes down to the bone. Second: realists might deny that standard forms of ideal theory amount to a diagnosis of leukemia, a dangerous but treatable condition. To the extent that political moralism prescribes things for politics that the basic conditions and presuppositions of politics render permanently impossible, ideal theory is more like a doctor whose sole advice to patients is 'you are dying in the sense that all humans are mortal; my advice is to hope that science discovers the formula for eternal life.' Now, all human beings *are* mortal; and a patient (not to mention a doctor) who forgets this will make very poor medical choices. And no doubt *memento mori* is excellent spiritual discipline; a certain kind of moralism and a certain kind of realism can be fused in the form of an Augustinian outlook that sees human life as both fallen and fleeting. Still, the doctor whose *only* advice is spiritual is not much of a doctor; she does not treat illness and injury, as most of us think doctors should.

That may be the accusation that realists really mean to level at ideal theory. Fascinatingly – and the chance of realizing this is not the least valuable service of Estlund's piece – realists' main complaint may turn out to be that ideal theory contains too *much* deep wisdom, of the wrong kind, not too little. Realism may involve a willed and precise shallowness, a determination that certain moral graveyards should be treated as occasions not for mourning but for whistling past them. Geuss, in a passage cited by Hall and Sleat, describes the characteristic mood of much philosophy, with its unlikely, evangelistic faith that apparent moral and social chaos is ultimately consistent with an ordered and intelligible cosmos, as 'comedy without the humor' (Geuss 2014: 207). Realist political theory may involve, on the contrary, tragedy without the gloom.

## Future directions

This volume's contributions suggest several future directions for realism. They all have something to do with 'real politics,' but very different somethings: different from one another, and from the familiar, slightly polemical agenda that realism adopted in its youth.

First, real theory might pursue the question of feasibility across many different dimensions. Again, questions of external (and, depressingly, internal) security may represent the greatest practical limitations on ideal aspirations and the greatest potential source of deep wisdom regarding political truths that we often evade. But both practical and theoretical lessons may also be drawn from other obstacles that real politics places in the way of our best-laid ideals: e.g. the 'dirty hands' fact that bringing about good states of affairs may require moral wrongs; the ubiquity of scarcity and necessary trade-offs; the tension between cultural diversity and social equality; the ever-increasing constraints that environmental damage places on aspirations to human prosperity. Many of these questions are well known to political scientists and practical politicians but have been barely canvassed by high political theory – or else relegated to the realm of 'political ethics,' which is, not without reason, considered realism's close cousin but which realist political theory might do more to reconnect with.

Another, only slightly compatible direction of study would consist of doing political thought without the capital-h History, without the aspiration to happy endings and easy reconciliation. As noted above, one version of this – present in Hall and Sleat, Sabl and others, and reformulated, rather than rejected, by McQueen – involves an alternative canon, which would begin with Thucydides and Sophocles rather than Plato and culminate in a 'postwar theory' that places Niebuhr and Morgenthau ahead of Rawls. But another version could be called even more realist than that. It would start with the Machiavellian doubt that the only source of ideas is other ideas. It might on the contrary adopt the premise that the best political concepts largely reflect – while of course also influencing – political experience, embodied in history rather than theory. It might be time to rehabilitate a kind of political theory that resembles Machiavelli's *Discourses* more than Sidgwick's *Methods of Ethics* (Sabl, forthcoming).

This suggests a final mode of realism, one that would cast systematic (and admittedly paradoxical) doubt on the superiority of theory to practice. We all know of Wittgenstein's claim that words and concepts are characterized not by neat definitions but by family resemblances. The family surnamed Realism is a large and nontraditional one in which splits and remarriages are not unknown and many prospective partners raise eyebrows. One of the family's branches is profoundly philosophical, determined to delve deeply into unpleasant truths that may, at the limit, tempt us into counsels of despair. But another branch, also recognizably realist, is very different: slightly rough and streetwise. This latter branch of the family is not without its own wisdom, though it might not be a particularly theoretically minded form of wisdom. While its members may lack polish, old school ties, and the taste to paint (or want to paint) Justice in beautiful hues, they can usually be relied on to know what's what.

## Note

1. An important forthcoming work is Sleat 2017.

## Acknowledgements

Thanks are due to the Lee Kuan Yew School of Public Policy and the Department of Political Science at the National University of Singapore for generously supporting the workshop that led to this special issue.

## Disclosure statement

No potential conflict of interest was reported by the authors.

## References

Estlund, D. (2014). Utopophobia. *Philosophy and Public Affairs, 42*, 113–134.
Galston, W. A. (2010). Realism in political theory. *European Journal of Political Theory, 9*, 385–411.
Geuss, R. (2014). The wisdom of oedipus and the idea of a moral cosmos. In *A world without why* (pp. 195–222). Princeton, NJ: Princeton University Press.
MacIntyre, A. (1978). The end of ideology and the end of the end of ideology. In *Against the self-images of the age* (pp. 3–11). Notre Dame, IN: University of Notre Dame Press.
Rossi, E. (2016). Can realism move beyond a *Methodenstreit*? *Political Theory, 44*, 410–420.
Rossi, E., & Sleat, M. (2014). Realism in normative political theory. *Philosophy Compass, 9*, 689–701.
Sabl, A. (2015). Liberal realism: A realist theory of liberal politics. *Perspectives on Politics, 13*, 1141–1143.
Sabl, A. (in press). History and politics. In A. Coventry & A. Sager (Ed.), *The Humean mind*. London and New York: Routledge.
Sagar, R. (2011). Is ideal theory practical? *Review of International Studies, 37*, 1949–1965.

Sagar, R. (2013). *Secrets and leaks*. Princeton, NJ: Princeton University Press.
Sleat, M. (Ed.). (2017). *Politics recovered: Essays on realist political thought*. New York, NY: Columbia University Press.
Stears, M. (2007). Liberalism and the politics of compulsion. *British Journal of Political Science, 37*, 533–553.

# Ethics, morality and the case for realist political theory

Edward Hall and Matt Sleat

**ABSTRACT**
A common trait of all realistic political theories is the rejection of a conception of political theory as applied moral philosophy and an attempt to preserve some form of distinctively political thinking. Yet the reasons for favouring such an account of political theory can vary, a point that has often been overlooked in recent discussions by realism's friends and critics alike. While a picture of realism as first-and-foremost an attempt to develop a more practical political theory which does not reduce morality to politics is often cited, in this paper we present an alternative understanding in which the motivation to embrace realism is grounded in a set of critiques of or attitudes towards moral philosophy which then feed into a series of political positions. Political realism, on this account, is driven by a set of philosophical concerns about the nature of ethics and the place of ethical thinking in our lives. This impulse is precisely what motivated Bernard Williams and Raymond Geuss to their versions of distinctively realist political thought and is important to emphasise because it demonstrates that realism does not set politics against ethics (a misunderstanding typically endorsed by realism's critics) but is rather an attempt to philosophise about politics without relying on understandings of morality which we have little reason to endorse.

It is by now something of a platitude to remark that political realists resist the thought that political theory can be a form of applied moral philosophy and in so doing have the general ambition of preserving some autonomy for distinctively political thinking. However, while all those who have recently been involved in the renewed interest in some kind of realist political theorising share this commitment, their reasons for doing so vary and the fact that realists have come to political realism via different intellectual routes is frequently overlooked by some of realism's defenders but also by its many critics. While the different impulses that motivate the 'realist turn' in political theory ought not to be thought of as mutually exclusive, it is important to set them out independently from one another in order to adequately grasp the multifaceted nature of the contemporary realist current. Indeed, it is only when one truly understands what the different contemporary realist thinkers are trying to do that one can then begin to understand the distinctive contribution realism seeks to make to contemporary political theory – and this is an important step if one is to critically engage with realism on its own terms.

One impulse that motivates some realists is that of developing a more practical political theory whose closer proximity to the real world of politics, through a greater appreciation of feasibility constraints or sensitivity to the conditions of political possibility, makes it better suited as a guide to action for political agents as they actually are. From this perspective, the key failing of much contemporary political philosophy has been to abstract or idealise away too far from the real world, creating an unbridgeable gap between theory and practice.[1]

A second, more philosophically nuanced, impulse stems from the thought that politics has a character that cannot be sufficiently subsumed by morality, especially the ethical thought appropriate for reflecting upon individual behaviour, either because politics pursues ends that are sufficiently distinct from other areas of human life (such as order and stability), or because politics is inherently a collective rather than individual endeavour. Such a position does not pit politics against ethics but rather insists that there might be something appropriately called political ethics that is not simply the application of personal morality to the political sphere. This position does not commit realists to the thought that the demands of (non-political) morality have literally no place in politics, only that those demands do not have automatic or antecedent normative authority over political life.

Both of these motivations to realism stem from the basic thought that there is something specific about politics that needs to be reflected in any appropriately realistic political theory. Neither seeks a political theory cleansed of all moral content, but it is clear that the impulse to both of these kinds of realism comes through a concern for recovering what is specifically political from the tendency to subsume politics into moral philosophy. Importantly, these forms of realism do not necessarily have anything to say about the subject matter of moral philosophy as traditionally conceived beyond their rejection of the idea that the prevailing modes of moral philosophising can be seamlessly applied to the political sphere.

There is another possible impulse to realism, one that comes more directly via moral philosophy and which is grounded in a related set of critiques of contemporary moral philosophy which then feed into a series of political positions that are recognisably realist. It is distinctive of this motivation to endorse political realism that it depends upon certain substantive attitudes and concerns within moral philosophy, or maybe more precisely attitudes *towards* moral philosophy from the perspective of the ethical more broadly conceived. On this impulse, political realism is driven by a set of philosophical concerns about the nature of ethics and the place of ethical thinking in our lives.[2]

These three different impulses have tended to be somewhat elided in the contemporary literature; not only by realism's critics. A familiar view of what realism is for tends to be some combination of the first two impulses – to create a more relevant political theory that does not reduce politics to morality. This is not necessarily mistaken but it is not the entire story, especially because the third perspective we have introduced is precisely the impulse that (even allowing for the differences between them) motivated both Bernard Williams and Raymond Geuss, the two most influential thinkers in contemporary realism, to versions of distinctively realist political thought. Though it is not wrong to think that Williams or Geuss were concerned about the issue of feasibility constraints, nor that they sought a more distinctively political form of thinking about politics, they arrived at those positions via the route of considerations that are properly thought of as part of ethical thought.

It is important to emphasise this now as confusion about what realism is for – why we need realist political thought – is to a large extent responsible for the frequent misunderstanding (typically endorsed by realism's critics) that realism hankers for a political theory that eschews all ethical content. The impulse to realism that we wish to highlight here points rather to the fact that it's most recent instantiation in political theory grew out of specifically ethical concerns, and in particular the attempt to think philosophically about politics from a particular ethical standpoint.[3] Realism on this reading does not set politics against ethics *per se*; instead it is an attempt to philosophise about politics without relying on understandings of morality which we have little reason to endorse.

\*\*\*

That there might be some uncertainty about what realism is for and the needs to which it responds will likely look strange given the quantity of survey articles that have already been published which address this question directly. But it might be that these are part of the problem. While Bernard Williams' *In the Beginning was the Deed* was published in 2005 and Raymond Geuss' *Philosophy and Real Politics* in 2008, it was the publication of William Galston's 'Realism in Political Theory' in 2010 that in many ways marked the start of the realist discussion in the discipline as whole. Galston's piece weaved together a myriad of otherwise very disparate theorists into a tapestry that could plausibly be called realist, and in doing so help set a research agenda for realism that it has largely followed since. Realism is presented 'as an alternate to ideal theory'; an attack on the 'high-liberalism' of Rawls and Dworkin; a rejection of utopianism, moralism, hypothetical consent, universal principles and the priority of justice. According to Galston, realists urge us to focus on the distinctiveness of the political; the ways that institutions actually function; the motivations that people actually have; the importance of order and stability; the contingency of all political arrangements; the limits of political possibility; and the ubiquity of conflict and disagreement. What is realism for? It is, we are told, for correcting the excesses of ideal normative theorising by drawing our attention to an 'experience-based concept of feasibility' (Galston 2010, pp. 400–401) which will enable normative political theory to finally get the ear of policy-makers and have the sort of 'impact' on the real world that it has long hankered for.

Since Galston's article there have been several further reviews or surveys of the realist literature, all of which carve the intellectual terrain up differently but generally stress something like this view of realism, and Williams and Geuss remain constant throughout as the intellectual figureheads of this movement in contemporary political theory.[4] While we do not want to deny that Williams and Geuss deserve this place in the recent realist pantheon, their inclusion as advocates *of this sort* of realism is problematic. When Williams and Geuss were developing their respective realisms were they really developing it simply in order to construct a more politically feasible form of theorising, or was there a different intellectual impulse behind their turn to political realism?

Speaking of Williams and Geuss together in this way necessarily overlooks some very significant differences between them. We do not wish to deny the existence of these and indeed will return to some of them later, but from a suitable level of generality they have much in common and it is this that we wish to focus on initially here.[5] They are unquestionably united in their deep scepticism, if not outright rejection, of most forms of modern moral philosophy, and certainly those we have inherited from Plato, Aristotle, Christianity, Kant and utilitarians such as Jeremy Bentham. This is sometimes the result of worries about specific features of these philosophies, such as Williams' charge that utilitarianism cannot make sense of the value of integrity or Geuss' worry that Kantianism misconceives of morality as a 'rule-guided activity'.[6] But often, and here they draw inspiration from Nietzsche whom both appreciated as a thinker of tremendous (if underappreciated) significance,[7] they were concerned more with identifying the most basic and often shared but implicit assumptions of modern moral philosophy that gave it its problematic character – especially insofar as it fails to make sense of the essential untidiness and complexities of our lived ethical experiences.[8] So we find both Williams and Geuss rejecting the possibility of fully distinguishing the moral from a non-moral point of view; the thought that morality is best understood as the impartial application of rational principles; and doubting the overriding authority of rationality (and philosophy more generally) in human lives.[9]

The philosophical import of these criticisms is best grasped by focusing on the distinction between ethics and morality Williams draws and his related rejection of 'morality, the peculiar institution'; the unquestioned framework within which most contemporary philosophers approach the study of ethics. Morality is 'a particular development of the ethical', one which 'emphasises certain ethical notions rather than others ... and it has some peculiar presuppositions' (1985, p. 6). In particular, Williams criticises the role that morality gives to the ideas of moral obligation and blame at the expense of other things such as our dispositions, moral sentiments and the thick ethical concepts that give life meaning and purpose (1985; Chapter 10). In addition, morality hopes to rescue moral value from contingency and this encourages it to emphasise a series of idealised contrasts 'between force and reason, persuasion and rational convictions, shame and guilt, dislike and disapproval, mere rejection and blame' (1985, pp. 194–195). Williams and Geuss both deny that the aspiration to achieve such a pure moral theory is coherent because they insist that we cannot study the subject matter of ethics 'without constantly locating it within the rest of human life, and without unceasingly reflecting on the relations one's claims have with history, sociology, ethnology, psychology and economics' (Geuss, 2008, p. 7). To this end Williams holds, and Geuss's insistence that we must think *outside* the prevailing models of moral understanding shows that he agrees, that philosophers are mistaken in thinking that 'morality just is the ethical in a rational form' (1995a, p. 246). By forgetting this, Williams alleges that morality has pernicious implications for ethical life because it 'makes people think that without its very special obligation, there is only inclination; without its utter voluntariness, there is only force; without its ultimately pure justice, there is no justice' (1985, p. 196).

Neither Williams nor Geuss thought that their scepticism about modern moral philosophy implied some disabling moral scepticism or nihilism because neither thought philosophy stood in that sort of foundational role to ethical life. Rather, ethics is a deeply socially embedded and practical activity: a matter of acting in accordance with a set of internalised dispositions which are the result of a 'very complex historical deposit' (Williams, 1995b, p. 189). Although philosophy is devoid of the sort of 'force' that might compel someone to act in the ways that many philosophers insist morality demands, it does not obviously follow that this recognition must unseat our ethical dispositions and sentiments. Yet because there is, in Williams's terminology, no 'Archimedean Point' from which we can argue the amoralist into moral life,[10] we ought to accept that philosophy, if it can be of any help at all, has to start from within moral experience and so cannot ground it.[11] The aim of moral philosophy is 'to sharpen perception, to make one more acutely and honestly aware of what one is saying, thinking and feeling' (Williams, 1993a, p. xv). What philosophy cannot claim to do is to provide a perspective from which we are able to transcend our history and experience to rationally validate particular moral practices because there is no 'absolutist Platonic conception of the world' from which we can make such judgements (Geuss, 2005a, p. 4). In this sense, no moral philosophy is going to do the sort of justificatory work that has so often been demanded of it. However, philosophical reflection can aid self-understanding by helping us to appreciate where our commitments and values might be the result of self-deception, metaphysical illusions or social deceit. This kind of self-understanding undermines certain intellectualised pictures of ethics and this has important ramifications for practice because morality 'is a deeply rooted and still powerful misconception of life' (Williams, 1985, p. 196).[12]

Williams and Geuss are not alone in contemporary philosophy in their holding out little hope for a philosophical understanding of morality that can provide an ultimate justification of a particular form of ethical life or a set of 'universal' moral principles. Acknowledging the socially embedded nature of moral thinking should lead us to acknowledge that 'we do not make our thoughts out of nothing; they come in part from what is around us, and we have a very poor grasp, of what their source may be' (Williams, 2007c, p. 327). Yet this appreciation of the limits of our philosophical understanding does not lead Williams or Geuss to hold that we must therefore abandon the hope of achieving any kind of more reasoned comprehension of our commitments (or indeed ourselves), even if they think it should give us pause. It does, however, force us to pose some potentially unsettling questions. Thus Geuss insists that once we accept that 'the Cartesian project of setting aside everything we know and value and starting *ab nihilo* to build up our own views about the world on a certain and incontrovertible base that owes nothing to social conventions is unworkable', the most pertinent question we have to ask is 'to what extent is it possible for us to free ourselves from our own illusions and work our way towards a realistic, or at least more realistic, worldview' (Geuss, 2010c, p. x). Attaining such a worldview is the basic precondition of making any sense of our lives here and now.

Williams and Geuss both grappled with this question in some detail and recognised that it had important ramifications for the dominant form political philosophy had taken in the late twentieth century, what Williams called 'political moralism' and Geuss 'politics as applied ethics'. As they saw it, this approach holds that politics has its theoretical and normative foundation in some external non-political moral system or set of values which then provide the justification for a particular form of political life. In liberal political theory this often takes the form of relying upon something like a neo-Kantian account of the autonomous individual and from that justifying specifically liberal institutions and practices. Politics is grounded in morality and political philosophy is but a sub-branch of moral philosophy. Yet if morality cannot be all it has purported to be not only does this undermine traditional moral philosophies, it also throws into severe doubt any political theory that takes itself to be grounded in those philosophies. Accordingly, one of the reasons why politics cannot be applied ethics is because ethics cannot be applied ethics. If we continue to think that politics is a form of 'applied ethics' then the problems that we encounter in making sense of morality are only going to replicate themselves at the level of politics.

So how should we understand politics and our political commitments if we accept that they are not grounded in an ahistorical, objective, universal morality? And how might we stabilise our political beliefs without falling into a crude relativism or anihilism of political abandonment?

From the 1980s through to his death in 2007, Richard Rorty offered his own contentious anti-foundationalist response to this question which he called liberal ironism (Rorty, 1989). To be a liberal ironist is to be someone who is fully aware of the contingent nature of their beliefs that they cannot be universally justified to all people, but who manages to cling to them by adopting a spirit of ironic wonder. Neither Williams nor Geuss were satisfied with Rorty's answer, yet it haunted them both. In the last decades of his life Williams made several attempts to distinguish his position, both philosophically and politically, from Rorty's: Rorty is one of the main 'deniers', those who reject that truth has any value, that Williams sought to refute in *Truth and Truthfulness*, and liberal irony is the object of some scorn in *In the Beginning was the Deed*.[13] Geuss, who admits that he spent more time thinking about Rorty than anyone else outside his small circle of intimates, characteristically focuses more on his political differences with Rorty, though those seem underlined by a worry that there might be a connection between a rejection of traditional philosophical endeavours and endorsing American patriotism (Geuss, 2010d). The lack of seriousness with which most moral and political philosophers have taken Rorty's anti-foundationalism stands in contrast with the significance that Williams and Geuss gave him. And one plausible reason for this is that Rorty matters to Williams and Geuss insofar as they shared his sense of the philosophical problem of making sense of ourselves in modernity.

What unites Williams and Geuss' response to the problem of anti-foundationalism was a turn to truthful, realistic reflections on our existing practices in the hope that we might be able to find in them adequate basis for our beliefs or grounds for ethical, social and political critique. For Williams, the basic legitimation demand falls out of the very practice of politics itself – rule through legitimated power (Williams, 2005, p. 5). Likewise, we can understand basic human rights violations and even certain forms of minimal liberalism as supported by basic facts of the activity of politics (Williams, 2005, pp. 62–74). Geuss' background in critical theory led him in a quite different direction: while he warns us that 'what is "out there" is usually a farrago of truths, half-truths, misperceptions, indifferent appearance, and illusion that needs to be seriously processed before one can accept any of it as "real"'(2014a, p. 140), he still thought that with care reality can give us the grounds to engage in the critique of power, to see through extant political relations as the rule of one group over another, to unmask moral justifications as ideological niceties. We have no need for Rorty's ironism if reality gives us enough material to work with.

We might say therefore that the realist spirit is imbued with a certain ethic – the ethic of truthfulness, a willingness to see our political reality as it really is, to not succumb to illusions or wishful thinking or to imagine a greater fit between our needs, interests and values and the world than actually exists (Williams, 1993b, p. 166; Geuss, 2005c, p. 223). In this regard, part of the value of truthfulness lies with the thought that we have good reasons to 'want to understand who we are, to correct error, to avoid deceiving ourselves, [and] to get beyond comfortable falsehood' (Williams, 2002, p. 15). Or, in a characteristically more polemic tone, Geuss writes that we should

> try to become aware of the extent to which we presuppose certain values, and try to make our assumptions as realistic as possible. We can, that is, try to be as truthful and truth-loving as possible in developing an alternative to the deceitful, hypermoralised views of Plato, Aristotle, Kant, and the other major figures in the history of Western ethics. (2005c, p. 230)[14]

In large part it is this ethic of truthfulness that led Williams and Geuss to their realist political positions. Vitally, they both insist that a truthful account of ourselves and our ethical predicament requires us to endorse a more historical philosophical perspective. Here their debt to Nietzsche is clear even if his influence plays out in different ways in their work. For Geuss, to keep the real world in view requires one to think largely in terms of an ideological critique of existing power relations, and to remain forever sceptical and vigilant in the face of normative theories that claim to be grounded in rationality or morality but are really covers for more sectional interests. Precisely because the question of how power actually operates in a given context to influence our beliefs is deeply complex, Geuss insists that 'only a historical account of the particular details of the case will be at all enlightening' (2008, p. 51). Moreover, because power influences our ways of orienting ourselves to the world in myriad ways, the reflective philosopher must ask why certain issues are not being accorded the attention they deserve and why other issues are treated as having central significance (2008, p. 54).[15] Here historical reflection is again invaluable:

> the reasons why we have most of the political and moral concepts that we have (in the forms we have them) are contingent, historical reasons, and only a historical account will give us the beginnings of understanding of them and allow us to reflect critically on them rather than simply taking them for granted. (2008, p. 69).

Geuss' politics are difficult to pin down exactly. In part this is because he rejects, wholesale, the suggestion that political argument (or criticism) must be constructive, effectively insulating him (he thinks) from the need to offer fully worked out alternatives to the forms of liberal capitalism that Western European and North American states practice, which he so vehemently loathes (2010a, 2014d). It is also because of the difficulty of adequately grasping the nature of his response to liberalism. In 'Liberalism and its discontents', Geuss suggests that even if the Kantian inspired strands are non-starters we might be able to vindicate the strand of liberalism 'that is action-oriented but reflexively anti-utopian and [which] asserts that no system either of action or thought is perfect' (2005c, p. 28). More recently, however, Geuss has dismissed Rawlsian liberalism as the political-philosophical equivalent of 'trickle-down' economics, declaring that its central purpose is to allow 'people who observe great inequality in their societies to continue to feel good about themselves, provided that they support some cosmetic forms of redistribution'. And regardless of the gloss that liberal philosophers may put on it (and here Geuss's condemnation seemingly applies beyond Rawls to all self-avowed liberals) the fact is that modern capitalism is nothing more than a rotten prison.

> A prison warden may put on a benevolent smile (Rawls) or a grim scowl (Ayn Rand) … [but] that is a mere result of temperament, mood, calculation and the demands of the immediate situation: the fact remains that he is the warden of the prison, and, more importantly, that the prison is a prison. To shift attention from the reality of the prison to the morality, the ideals and the beliefs of the warden is an archetypical instance of an ideological effect. (Geuss, 2016)

As a result, even though it is very hard for us to think of politically plausible alternatives to capitalism, realists must avoid the temptation of distracting themselves from the task of unmasking the power relations present in their societies by refining their moral intuitions or setting them out in painstaking detail.

Like Geuss, Williams also urges us to recognise that we must attend to history 'if we are to know what reflective attitude to take to our own conceptions' (2006, p. 191). This is because some of the elements of our moral and political outlooks function, in a Wittgensteinian sense, like fixed points around which the rest of our arguments revolve. Hence, Williams claims that our belief that 'every citizen, indeed every human being … deserves equal consideration', is best understood not as a 'propositional belief than the schema of various arguments'. But it does not therefore follow that it is sufficient to make as much sense of our moral and political outlooks from the inside as we can. Rather, the very fact that such fixed points can seem *unhintergehbar* means that if we are to adopt the correct reflective attitude towards our own conceptions we have to ask a series of historical questions because such an understanding alone can help us to 'distinguish between different ways in which various of our ideas and procedures can seem to be such that we cannot get beyond them, that there is no conceivable alternative' (2006, p. 195).[16] This is why Williams insists that while one cannot in good faith reproach liberal political philosophers for not seeing beyond the outer limits of what they find acceptable, one can reproach them for not being 'interested enough in why this is so, in why their most basic convictions should seem to be … simply there' (2006, p. 197).[17]

Williams also insists that while it is simply a fantasy to think that all of our current conceptions, beliefs and forms or arguing for them will continue to make sense to us when we take his scepticism about philosophy and the morality system seriously, there is equally no reason to assume that they will all be discredited. Indeed, as we have argued elsewhere (Hall, 2014), Williams was adamant that a form of liberalism associated with Judith Shklar's liberalism of fear, extricated from the thick metaphysical and moral assumptions of previous justifications, could be vindicated in modernity (Williams, 2005, pp. 1–17; Sagar, 2016). This is because although Williams was deeply impressed by aspects of Nietzsche's critique of morality, he rejected the suggestion that 'our growing understanding that the world has no metaphysical structure whatsoever' *must* also discredit liberal ideas of humanitarianism, equality and freedom (2007a, p. 316). Although his scepticism about the morality system may have discredited the grounds upon which moralised conceptions of liberalism are built, he insists that if we focus on the nature of politics and the basic legitimation demand that is internal to it, we can find sufficient reason to continue to endorse a version of liberal politics because it alone can realistically claim to help people here and now avoid what is universally feared: 'torture, violence, arbitrary power, and humiliation' (2002, p. 265).

Williams's attempt to sketch a realist defence of actually existing liberalism generated a rather scornful response from Geuss, who accused Williams of paddling about in the 'tepid and slimly puddle created by Locke, J.S. Mill and Isaiah Berlin' (2014b, p. 184). It is, however, worth noting that this is (fittingly) not really best understood as a philosophical dispute but as a divergence in political and historical judgement. Geuss insists that Williams's (purported) optimism about finding meaning in our social world is not something that should be taken for granted and muses on the divergence between himself and Williams in this respect by remarking that Williams 'was a man who was remarkably comfortable in his own skin, and who fitted in easily with the existing world of politics and academic society, despite his high scepticism about many of the purported theoretical pillars of that world' (2014b, p. 189).

Whether or not this kind of psychological speculation is helpful or accurate is not for us to decide, although it is worth noting that Williams does not deny that 'there are very compelling true accounts of the world that could lead anyone to despair who did not hate humanity' (2002, p. 268) and this hardly strikes us as the kind of statement the naively or wilfully optimistic would countenance. It is true, though, that Williams's political thought retains a judgment that although we might still be struggling to make sense of our moral and political practices the prospect remains of a coherent and plausible genealogical account of our politics which is not thoroughly debunking. Geuss on the other hand has seemingly fully resigned himself to the incoherent and fractured nature of life in modernity:

> The only possible meaning you could give your life in the twentieth century that is minimally realistic is to resist the social pressures towards uniformity and homogeneity in all areas, and to struggle against the subordination of human subjectivity and individual life to the demands of the maximisation of return on capital ... even a 'bitter' happiness is not nothing and in any case it is probably all we have left. (2014e, pp. 108–110)

Such utter pessimism and resignation stands in contrast to Williams's political thought, no doubt intentionally so. Nevertheless, the importance lies in the fact that these are both attempts to try and make sense of our political and moral condition in a disenchanted world. The turn to the realities of political life is a response to the fact that we can no longer truthfully yearn for an escape from the contingencies of politics via the permanence and stability of morality.

\*\*\*

We hope that it is by now clear why Williams and Geuss rejected the idea that political theorists must begin by articulating an empirically abstemious and systematic ideal ethical theory which can then mechanically be applied to the political world (Geuss, 2008, pp. 6–7). Their point is not merely that such an approach fails to operate with the kind of experientially grounded conception of feasibility. It is rather that this cannot be the right way to think about politics because there is little reason to think that we can construct such a pure ethical theory in the first place. Yet despite their scepticism of modern conceptions of 'morality' and the received understanding of its relationship to political practice, it is a mistake to think that their political realisms are committed to thinking that prescriptive political argument should eschew the use of first-order ethical claims or avoid appealing to moral values *tout court*. In *Philosophy and Real Politics* Geuss is especially clear on this score: 'nothing in this book should be taken to imply that no one should ever allow normative considerations of any kind to play any role whatever in deciding to act politically' (2008, p. 99).

This comes out especially clearly by focusing on how to theorise in terms of Williams's basic legitimation demand. As noted earlier, Williams attempts to articulate a freestanding conceptual distinction between politics and mere domination which can ground our attempt to reflect normatively on politics without making the mistake of thinking that politics is reducible to morality. The fact that politics exists to solve the first political question, and that the state's claim to be acting legitimately rests on the recognition of the governed, enables us to evaluate the actions of states from a normative perspective without merely applying an antecedently justified ideal moral theory to the political domain.[18] Williams accordingly rejects the '*basic* relation of morality to politics as being that represented either by the enactment model or the structural model' whereby the former seeks to enact prior moral principles in practice (such as utilitarianism) and the latter wants to structure politics through limiting what counts as rightful political action by pre-political moral principles (2005, p. 2). However, he is also at pains to point out that his realism recognises that 'there can be local applications of moral ideas in politics, and these may take, on a limited scale, an enactment or structural form' (2005, p. 8). This follows when we recognise that when we ask whether or not we should continue to comply with our state's demands we will only answer in the affirmative if we think it satisfies the basic legitimation demand. The (often tacit) legitimation story must 'make sense' (MS) – and when we ask what makes sense to us here and now we are posing a normative question because 'what (most) MS to us is a structure of authority which we think we should accept'. Thinking in these terms therefore requires us to engage in 'first order discussions using our political, moral, social, interpretative, and other concepts' (2005, p.11). The key point, however, is that these moral ideas have to be understood in a way that is congruent with

Williams and Geuss' sceptical remarks about the morality system. This means that there is no reason to think that moral reasons will always trump all other reasons in play. Moreover, their brand of political realism advises against any complacency as to which moral ideas we can help ourselves to in the attempt to make sense of our political lives, for many of the moral ideas that contemporary political philosophers utilise may 'no longer do what they once did or us; some of them may not, in honest reflection, now be credible' (Williams, 2014b, p. 317). Geuss gives an especially illustrative example of such realist theorising when criticising political theories which assume that one can start theorising by treating certain moral concepts like rights as foundational, as Nozick does, without engaging in an historical analysis of why we think this is appropriate here and now (2008, pp. 60–70).

In addition, they both think that the political credibility of our first-order arguments depends on whether or not such ideas actually make political sense in our historical and political context. Once we grant that 'politics is in the first instance about action and the contexts of action', we ought also to acknowledge that 'if one wants understanding or any kind of guidance for action, one will have to take the specific cultural and historical circumstances into consideration' (Geuss, 2008, pp. 11 + 14). In this sense political philosophy must appeal to resources that moral reflection cannot provide by itself. This commitment drives Williams's (under-appreciated) papers on liberty where he argues that a workable political conception of liberty has to be constructed from a non-political conception of freedom and yet be 'socially presentable' where that means it must be compatible with a realistic assessment of political and practical possibility (Williams, 2001). For these reasons, his realism is committed to the view that social and historical interpretation is not an optional extra that political theorists can choose to engage *if* they want to think about how to their pure moral principles might be applied. Instead, this kind of reflection plays an ineliminable role in the articulation of our political values and commitments (Hall, in press). This illustrates that moralism is not the only vice realists seek to avoid; wishful thinking is just as, if not more, politically and philosophically problematic. Williams and Geuss both think that they only way to avoid this vice is by reflecting unsentimentally, honestly and truthfully, even though the truths about our political situation that they seek to reveal sometimes conflict quite sharply.

This is in an important sense to be expected, for such differences are properly to be thought of as contestable interpretative claims about the political world we inhabit and are exactly the sort of disputes that we should recognise and wish to preserve as political. Furthermore, they are both good enough philosophers – and good enough Nietzscheans – to know that there is no 'standpoint from which our representations as whole could be measured against the world as (in this sense) it really is' (Williams, 2002, p. 17). Only very crude conceptions of political realism will forget this (Geuss, 2005a, p. 4). We can adjudicate between competing interpretations, most notably because some interpretations will not be adequately responsive to the demands of truthfulness. The key point is that for both Williams and Geuss the endeavour to avoid wishful thinking is exactly what realism demands even when doing so is difficult for us because it may problematise some of our most cherished political ideas or undermine the likelihood that they might be realised any time soon. This impulse is the beating heart of Williams and Geuss' realisms. Their work sees the need to be truthful as a kind of 'ethical necessity' which needs intellectual courage (Williams, 2002, p. 15) because they both think that if we do not 'face the world truthfully, any hope for a better politics will be doomed' (Williams, 2007c, p. 329).

This is why there is some inevitable indeterminacy about precisely what this strand of political realism demands. The insistence that we must speak truthfully about politics and the role that morality plays in political argument is elusive. However, grasping this clarifies why realism cannot accurately be characterised as a purely negative, or critically spasmodic, reaction to everything neo-Kantian. Rather, at its best realism offers glimpses of an alternative, constructive, way of doing political philosophy if one is sceptical of the prevailing conceptions of morality we have inherited. And while any coherent realism recognises that prescriptive realist political arguments will inevitably be ethically laden in various ways, contrary to what some of its least charitable critics imply (Erman & Moller, 2015), this is not something realists should be embarrassed about (much less does it show that the realist project is self-refuting).

\*\*\*

The impulse that drove Williams and Geuss to adopt variations of realistic approaches to understanding politics was not primarily dissatisfaction with how little 'impact' normative political theory has had, but rather how the realities of politics might help us make better sense of our political lives in a modern world in which the traditional certainties of morality and religion are no longer available to us. What is at stake is not how appeals to reality might close the gap between theory and practice, but how (if at all) reality might help stabilise our ethical and political beliefs in a disenchanted world. This *is* an ethical question in the broadest sense. It is wrong, therefore, to think that the point of realism is to find an amoral perspective from which we can begin doing pure political thinking unhampered by morality or normative thinking more generally. The driving impulse behind both Williams and Geuss' realism is the attempt to find an *ethical* position from which to reflect on politics once we truly recognise the manner in which the frameworks of moral thought which we have inherited – Aristotelian, Christian, Kantian and Utilitarian – cannot make adequate sense of our ethical and political lives. But it remains an open question, to which Williams and Geuss had different answers, as to what kind of politics we can affirm in the aftermath of such a critique.

## Notes

1. For such a reading see Valentini (2012). For scepticism that such 'non-ideal' theory ought to be understood as a form of realism see Sleat (2016).
2. Some recent work engages in this endeavour of making explicit the ethical commitments or motivations behind realist political thought. See Hall (2014), Owen (in press), Nye (2015), and Sagar (2016).
3. We are not attributing this intellectual impulse to all realists (either those who have been attributed the label or freely self-identify).
4. See Baderin (2014), Freeden (2012), Philp (2012), Rossi and Sleat (2014), Runciman (2012), and Scheuerman (2013).
5. The differences between Williams and Geuss are often significant but this paper seeks to paint a big picture in little space, and we think that the commonalities are worth noting in order to elucidate our point that realism is not necessarily best understood in the terms in which it is often presented.
6. See in particular, Geuss, 2010b; 2005c and Williams, 1993b, 1973.
7. Williams, for example, writing in 1981, declared that 'It is certain, even if not everyone has yet come to see it, that Nietzsche was the greatest moral philosopher of the past century. This was, above all, because he saw how totally problematical morality, as understood over many centuries, has become, and how complex a reaction that fact, when fully understood, requires' (2014b, p. 183). Geuss has written a large number of well-received essays on Nietzsche's thought: see especially 1994, 1997, 2005c, 2014c. For Williams's key discussions see (2002, 2007a, 2007b, 2007c, 2007d) which is deeply indebted to Nietzsche in a number of ways.
8. Insofar as Ancient Greek tragedy was 'realistic' in the sense that 'it is about people (eventually) facing up to the dire situations in which they actually find themselves without flinching and making difficult choices', Geuss insists that 'Philosophy is not the "natural" successor of tragedy but, if anything, of comedy. It is a kind of comedy without the humour' (2014f, p. 207).
9. Williams, 1985; Chapter 4 and 1981. See also Geuss (2010b).
10. Williams, 1985; chapter 2 and 1993a; Chapter 1.
11. This is why Williams is adamant that 'one's initial responsibilities [when approaching moral philosophy] should be to moral phenomena, as grasped in one's own experience and imagination', (1993a, p. xxi).
12. For Williams the most important ramification being an unmasking of the alienating moral perspectives the morality system favours which encourage us to experience ethical life in terms of fulfilling obligations (Williams, 1985; Chapter 10). The other key implication of Williams's view is wonderfully put by Nakul Krishna in the following terms: 'the world, Williams thought, is full of temptations to take simple moral views – everything from "bomb Iraq" to "maximise the good" – because the longer route of self-understanding and critique is hard, uncertain and risky. If philosophy can help us with any of this, it won't be because it discovers a formula to replace the traditional sources of moral understanding … but because it helps to improve the reflective self-understanding of those who have more, much more, to their lives than philosophy' (Krishna, 2016). Geuss thinks that loosening the hold of such a view of ethics matters precisely because it forms the 'tacit background of thinking and debate' in the modern world. Hence his insistence that getting outside ethics is 'an exceptionally good way to contribute to further human enlightenment' (2005a, 4 + 10).

13. Williams, 2002; passim. The basic problem Williams has with Rorty's ironism lies in his insistence that the ironist posture is 'itself still under the shadow of universalism' because it suggests that you cannot really believe in anything unless you endorse the kind of universalist moral grounding we cannot have: (2005, p. 67). For discussion of this see Hall (2014) and Sagar (2016). Geuss on the other hand rejects Rorty's ironism because he sees it as the philosophy of bookish intellectuals who 'do not pressingly have to act'. In this regard, he insists that 'irony will not allow the right kind of theoretically reflective, engaged political practice' (2005b, p. 27).
14. Like Geuss, Williams denies that Aristotle's approach can help us to make sense of our ethical lives in modernity. However, while Williams is sceptical of the attempt to ground ethical life in considerations about human nature – he notes that 'it is hard to believe that an account of human nature … will adequately determine one kind of ethical life among others' (1985, p. 52), precisely because the pervasively reflective nature of modernity has shown that 'there are various forms of human excellence which do not fit together in one harmonious whole (p. 153) – he is equally adamant that Aristotle's project 'at least makes sense; that it operates, so to speak, in the right corner of the field' (1996, p. 213).
15. Hence Geuss's (deeply controversial) contention) that Rawls' work is ideological insofar as it 'draws our attention *away* from the phenomenon of power and the way in which it influences our lives and the way we see the world' by getting us to focus instead on our intuitions on what is 'just' (2008, p. 90).
16. Geuss claims that philosophers inspired by Nietzsche and Wittgenstein acknowledge that 'at a certain point inquiry into the relevant context of human thought and action simply stops … [this means] that at some point we will simply encounter *facta bruta*, either expressions of human volition (will), natural phenomena, or human practices embedded in historically … contingent assumptions' (Geuss, 2010a, p. 182).
17. This informs Williams more general complaint that moralistic liberalism 'has a poor account, or in many cases no account, of the cognitive status of its own history' and no answer 'to the question of why what it takes to be the true moral solution to the questions of politics, liberalism, should for the first time (roughly) become evident in European society from the late seventeenth century onward' (2005, p. 9). This claim is obviously more problematic when thinking about Rawls' later work than the approaches favoured by thinkers like Nagel and Dworkin.
18. For further discussion see Hall (2015), Sagar (2016), and Sleat (2014).

## Acknowledgements

Earlier versions of this paper were presented at the 'Realisms and Moralisms' workshop at UCL and the 'What is Realism?' conference at the National University of Singapore. We are very grateful to all participants for their comments. Robert Jubb, Nakul Krishna, Andrew Sabl and Paul Sagar also kindly read and commented on a written draft and we benefited a lot from their advice. We would also like to thank an anonymous reader for CRISPP.

## Disclosure statement

No potential conflict of interest was reported by the authors.

## References

Baderin, A. (2014). Two forms of realism in political theory. *European Journal of Political Theory, 13*, 132–153.

Erman, E., & Moller, N. (2015). Political legitimacy in the real normative world: The priority of morality and the autonomy of the political. *British Journal of Political Science, 45*, 215–233.

Freeden, M. (2012). Interpretative realism and prescriptive realism. *Journal of Political Ideologies, 17*(1), 1–11.

Galston, W. (2010). Realism in political theory. *European Journal of Political Theory, 9*, 385–411.

Geuss, R. (1994). Nietzsche and genealogy. *European Journal of Philosophy, 2*, 274–292.

Geuss, R. (1997). Nietzsche and morality. *European Journal of Philosophy, 5*, 1–20.

Geuss, R. (2005a). Introduction. *Outside ethics* (pp. 1–10). Oxford: Princeton University Press.

Geuss, R. (2005b). Liberalism and its discontents. *Outside Ethics* (pp. 11–28). Oxford: Princeton University Press.

Geuss, R. (2005c). Thucydides, Nietzsche and Williams. In *Outside Ethics* (pp. 40–66). Oxford: Princeton University Press.

Geuss, R. (2008). *Philosophy and real politics*. Princeton: Princeton University Press.

Geuss, R. (2010a). Bourgeois philosophy and criticism. In *Politics and the imagination* (pp. 167–186). Oxford: Princeton University Press.

Geuss, R. (2010b). On the Very idea of a metaphysics of right. *Politics and the imagination* (pp. 43–60). Oxford: Princeton University Press.

Geuss, R., (2010c). Preface. In *Politics and the imagination* (pp. vii–xvi). Oxford: Princeton University Press.

Geuss, R. (2010d). Richard Rorty at Princeton – Personal reflections. In *Politics and the imagination* (pp. 151–163). Oxford: Princeton University Press.

Geuss, R. (2014a). A note on lying. In *A World without Why* (pp. 135–143). Oxford: Princeton University Press.

Geuss, R. (2014b). Did Williams do Ethics? In *A World without Why* (pp. 175–194). Oxford: Princeton University Press.

Geuss, R. (2014c). Marxism and the ethos of the twentieth century. In *A World without Why* (pp. 45–67). Oxford: Princeton University Press.

Geuss, R. (2014d). Must criticism be constructive? In *A World without Why* (pp. 68–90). Oxford: Princeton University Press.

Geuss, R. (2014e). The loss of meaning on the left. *A World without Why* (pp. 91–111). Oxford: Princeton University Press.

Geuss, R. (2014f). Wisdom of Oedipus and the Idea of a Moral Cosmos. In *A World without Why* (pp. 195–222). Oxford: Princeton University Press.

Geuss, R. (2016). *The idea of a critical theory*. Retrieved February 23, 2016, from http://thepointmag.com/2014/politics/idea-critical-theory.

Hall, E. (2014). Contingency, confidence and liberalism in the political thought of Bernard Williams. *Social Theory and Practice, 40*, 545–569.

Hall, E. (2015). Bernard Williams and the basic legitimation demand: A defence. *Political Studies, 63*, 466–480.

Hall, E. (in press). How to do realistic political theory (and why you might want to). *European Journal of Political Theory* doi:http://dx.doi.org/10.1177/1474885115577820

Krishna, N. 2016. *Add your own egg*. Retrieved February 17, 2016, from http://thepointmag.com/2016/examined-life/add-your-own-egg

Nye, S. (2015). Real politics and metaethical baggage. *Ethical Theory and Moral Practice, 18*, 1083–1100.

Owen, D. (in press). Realism in ethics and politics: Bernard Williams, political theory and the critique of morality. In M. Sleat (Ed.), *Politics recovered: Essays on realist political theory*. New York, NY: Columbia University Press.

Philp, M. (2012). Realism without illusions. *Political Theory, 40*, 629–649.

Rorty, R. (1989). *Contingency, irony, and solidarity*. Cambridge: Cambridge University Press.

Rossi, E., & Sleat, M. (2014). Realism in normative political theory. *Philosophy Compass, 9*, 689–701.

Runciman, D. (2012). What is realistic political philosophy? *Metaphilosophy, 43*, 58–70.

Sagar, P. (2016). From scepticism to liberalism? Bernard Williams, the foundations of liberalism and political realism *Political Studies, 64*, 368–384.

Scheuerman, W. (2013). The realist revival in political philosophy, or: Why new is not always improved. *International Politics, 50*, 798–814.

Sleat, M. (2014). Legitimacy in realist thought: Between moralism and realpolitik. *Political Theory, 42*, 314–337.

Sleat, M. (2016). Realism, liberalism and non-ideal theory. Or, are there two ways to do realistic political theory? *Political Studies, 64*, 27–41.

Valentini, L. (2012). Ideal vs. non-ideal theory: A conceptual map. *Philosophy Compass, 7*, 654–665.

Williams, B. (1973). A critique of utilitarianism. In *Utilitarianism: For and against* (pp. 75–150). Cambridge: Cambridge University Press.

Williams, B. (1981). Persons, character and morality. In *Moral Luck* (pp. 1–19). Cambridge: Cambridge University Press.

Williams, B. (1985). *Ethics and the limits of philosophy*. London: Fontana.

Williams, B. (1993a). *Morality: An introduction to ethics*. Cambridge: Cambridge University Press.

Williams, B. (1993b). *Shame and necessity*. Berkeley, CA: University of California Press.

Williams, B. (1995a). Moral luck: A postscript. In *Making sense of humanity* (pp. 241–247). Cambridge: Cambridge University Press.

Williams, B. (1995b). What does intuitionism imply? In *Making sense of humanity* (pp. 182–191). Cambridge: Cambridge University Press.

Williams, B. (1996). History, morality, and the test of reflection. In C. Korsgaard (Ed.), *The sources of normativity* (pp. 210–218). Cambridge: Cambridge University Press.

Williams, B. (2001). From freedom to liberty: The construction of a political value. *Philosophy & Public Affairs, 30*, 3–26.

Williams, B. (2002). *Truth and Truthfulness*. Oxford: Princeton University Press.

Williams, B. (2005). *In the beginning was the deed: Realism and moralism in political argument*, (ed. Geoffrey Hawthorn). Oxford: Princetion University Press.

Williams, B. (2006). Philosophy as humanistic discipline. In A. Moore (Ed.), *Philosophy as a humanistic discipline* (pp. 180–199). Oxford: Princeton University Press.

Williams, B. (2007a). Introduction to the gay science. In M. Burnyeat (Ed.), *The sense of the past: Essays in the history of philosophy* (pp. 311–324). Oxford: Princeton University Press.

Williams, B. (2007b). Nietzsche's minimalist moral psychology. In M. Burnyeat (Ed.), *The sense of the past: Essays in the history of philosophy* (pp. 299–310). Oxford: Princeton University Press.

Williams, B. (2007c). There are many kinds of eyes. In M. Burnyeat (Ed.), *The sense of the past: Essays in the history of philosophy* (pp. 325–330). Oxford: Princeton University Press.

Williams, B. (2007d). Unbearable suffering. In M. Burnyeat (Ed.), *The sense of the past: Essays in the history of philosophy* (pp. 331–340). Oxford: Princeton University Press.

Williams, B. (2014a). Review of '*Nietzsche on Tragedy*, by M.S. Silk and J.P. Stern; *Nietzsche: A Critical Life*, by Ronald Hayman; *Nietzsche*, vol. 1. *The Will to Power as Art*, by Martin Heidegger in his Essays and Reviews, 1959–2002, 179–183.

Williams, B. (2014b). The need to be sceptical. *Essays and reviews: 1959–2002* (pp. 311–317). Oxford: Princeton University Press.

# Political realism and the realist 'Tradition'

Alison McQueen

**ABSTRACT**
Appeals to a 'tradition' stretching back to Thucydides have been central to the recent emergence of realism in political theory. This article asks what work these appeals to tradition are doing and whether they are consistent with contemporary political realism's contextualist commitments. I argue that they are not and that realists also have independent epistemic reasons to attend to contextualist worries. Ultimately, I make the case for an account of the realist tradition that is at once consistent with moderate contextualist commitments and that preserves the classificatory and analytical value of tradition-building.

## 1. Introduction

Over the past decade, a collection of approaches grouped under the banner of 'political realism' has emerged as a challenge to liberal political theory (B. Williams, 2005; Geuss, 2008; Galston, 2010; Honig & Stears, 2011; Sleat, 2013; Rossi & Sleat, 2014). Most closely associated with the work of Raymond Geuss, Bernard Williams, and their followers, contemporary political realists have a standard account of their intellectual ancestry. Political realism, we are told, is a tradition of political thinking that was inaugurated in its secular form by Thucydides and in its Christian form by (St.) Paul and (St.) Augustine, carried into the modern era by Machiavelli, Hobbes, Hume, and Nietzsche, and sustained in the twentieth century by Weber and Schmitt (Mantena, 2012, pp. 455–456, Sleat, 2013, p. 2, Sigwart, 2013, pp. 409–410, Rossi & Sleat, 2014, p. 697).

This account prompts three observations. First, none of the thinkers listed self-identified as 'realists.' Second, the list excludes many who *did* so identify in the field of International Relations: classical realists like E.H. Carr and Hans Morgenthau, and more contemporary structural realists like Kenneth Waltz and John Mearsheimer. Third, realists' agreement on their intellectual ancestry has not yielded any consensus about realism's substantive commitments. This article focuses on the first observation (and, to a lesser extent, the second), particularly as they bear on the notion of a realist 'tradition'.[1] However, it is worth dwelling for a moment on the third observation. Even among its proponents, there is little agreement about what political realism is. It has been understood as a methodological critique, a disposition, a sensibility, a persuasion, and a distinctive conception of politics.

Here I define political realism, provisionally, as a family of approaches to the study, practice, and normative evaluation of politics that (a) affirms the autonomy (or, more minimally, the distinctiveness) of politics; (b) takes disagreement, conflict, and power to be ineradicable and constitutive features of politics; (c) rejects as 'utopian' or 'moralist' those approaches, practices, and evaluations which seem to deny these facts; and (d) prioritizes political order and stability over justice (or, more minimally, rejects the absolute priority of justice over other political values).[2]

In conceiving of realism as a *distinctive family* of approaches, I mean to emphasize both pieces of this phrase equally.[3] It is *distinctive* in the sense that there are other approaches and positions that reject these commitments (e.g. those found in Plato's *Republic* or John Rawls' *Theory of Justice*). It is a *family* of approaches in the sense that its various commitments can be developed and expressed along different lines. For instance, the commitment to the autonomy of politics might be developed along broadly Machiavellian lines to make the claim that politics is an amoral realm, or one with its own distinct normative rules, or one in which in which universal moral rules must be overridden and 'good' political actors must dirty their hands. Or the same commitment might be developed along less radical lines to make the claim that 'politics cannot be exhausted by morality and that key political concepts such as legitimacy and authority need to be rethought in conditions of ineradicable moral and political disagreement' (Rossi & Sleat, 2014, p. 691). Despite their differences, the approaches that emerge from these developmental trajectories bear a certain 'family resemblance' to one another.[4] The claims above, for instance, are all recognizably claims about the autonomy of politics.

While realism is a distinctive family of approaches, it is not a substantive *political position*: realists do not converge on the right rules and institutions for structuring our common life. Such commitments can only derive from a substantive political position (e.g. liberalism, socialism, republicanism, etc.) upon which realist commitments would then impose practical, methodological, and evaluative constraints.[5] Realism may also not be a substantive *political philosophy*. Consider the four public roles that Rawls (2001, pp. 2–4) thinks political philosophy might play. In each case, political realists must simply reject some of these roles or fulfill them only in a negative way (i.e. by ruling options out).

First, political philosophy fulfills a *practical role*: it helps us discover the basis for moral and political agreement about divisive issues or, barring that, at least provides some path for minimizing the scope of our differences. Many realists simply reject this difference-minimizing impulse, seeing it as a prelude to the displacement (Honig, 1993), repudiation (Morgenthau, 1946), or abolition (Gray, 1995) of politics (Sleat, 2014). Second, political philosophy fulfills an *orienting role*, by canvassing all possible individual, social and political ends and showing how they can cohere in 'a well-articulated conception of a just and reasonable society'(Rawls, 2001, p. 3). Once again, many realists would resist the impulse toward coherence and consistency here for reasons of deep value pluralism (Gray, 2000) or epistemic modesty about the powers of human rationality (Geuss, 2008). Many would also reject the abstraction and distancing implied by this conception of 'orientation' and insist instead that political philosophy should properly begin by attending to local and endogenous complaints (Pettit, 2015). Nevertheless, realists might contribute to this endeavor in a negative way by ruling certain political ends *out* (as unacceptably utopian, moralistic, perfectionist, etc.).

Third, political philosophy fulfills a *reconciling* role when it tries 'to calm our frustration and rage against our society and history by showing the way in which its institutions … developed over time as they did to attain their present, rational form' and by alerting us to the 'political good and benefits' of these institutions (Rawls, 2001, pp. 3–4). Absent any additional substantive political commitments (e.g. to liberalism, socialism, republicanism, etc.), realists would not be able to make a positive case for any actually existing institution. However, they could again contribute negatively to this effort at reconciliation by revealing many alternatives to our current institutions to be infeasible or dangerous. Finally, political philosophy fulfills a *realistically utopian* role by 'probing the limits of practicable political possibility' (Rawls, 2001, p. 4). This is the role of political philosophy in which the realist might seem to be most at home, as it is the role that most clearly invites negative and critical contributions. Yet, absent any substantive political commitments (in this case, liberal ones), one cannot imagine the realist making a positive contribution to the kind of substantive discussion Rawls has in mind – say, about the kind of democratic regime that is possible given the fact of reasonable pluralism. The larger lesson here is that one need not affirm the details of Rawls's particular account of the roles of political philosophy to conclude that political realism's core commitments make it more suited to ruling particular ends, principles, and alternatives out than to ruling them in.

Given this familial looseness and political and philosophical indeterminacy, realists' agreement on their intellectual ancestry is all the more striking. My suspicion is that these two facts are connected: they both result from realism's comparatively recent arrival on the scene of contemporary political theory (compare Condren, 1997, p. 47). Wanting to avoid being dismissed as a passing intellectual fad, political realists have been especially eager to construct a realist 'tradition' around a canon. And their lack of substantive agreement regarding their shared project has rendered political realists all the more eager to agree on their historical lineage.

That an assertion of tradition is comforting does not make it coherent. The first section of this article asks what work appeals to a tradition are doing for contemporary political realists. The second questions whether such appeals are consistent with realism's contextualist commitments. This question, I argue, bears crucially on realists' ability to learn from past thinkers. The third section proposes an account of the realist tradition (building on Bell, 2014) that can accommodate a certain contextualism while rejecting its most radical forms. Realists can retain the classificatory and analytical value of tradition-building without yielding to temptations to ignore what past 'realists' actually said.

## 2. The work of tradition

To see self-styled realists appealing to a 'realist tradition' and a canon of 'realist thinkers' might evoke déjà vu. Realism in postwar Anglo-American International Relations (IR) theory trod the same path. Writing in 1960, Martin Wight argued that IR lacked a canon of classic works. 'International theory, or what there is of it,' he concluded, 'is scattered, unsystematic, and mostly inaccessible to the layman. Moreover it is largely repellant and intractable in form' (Wight, 1960, pp. 37–38). In search of its own canon and traditions, the developing discipline of IR set about establishing a list of classic works reaching back to the Greco-Roman world (e.g. the selections in Brown, Nardin, and Rengger, 2002). This list was then divided and subdivided into various intellectual traditions.[6] Realists seemed to take to this tradition-building task with particular zeal, as many sought 'to construct a "realist" grand narrative in which historical figures with some affiliation to this mode of thought [were] lined up in a surreal identity parade of "the usual suspects"' (Murray, 1997, p. 3).

These canon-constructing and tradition-building efforts evoked a predictable set of interpretive criticisms from political and IR theorists.[7] First, these appeals to tradition work at a towering height of *abstraction*, as they inevitably must in order to link arguments from thinkers as diverse as Thucydides, Machiavelli, Hobbes, Carr, and Morgenthau 'across time and space' (Bell, 2009, p. 6, see also Boucher, 1998, pp. 16–19). Second, these appeals are highly *selective* in their appropriation of arguments, works, and thinkers. For instance, they tend to focus on Thucydides' Melian Dialog or Hobbes' description of the state of nature, with very little attention to the surrounding text or the thinker's broader corpus (Schmidt, 1998, pp. 26–29; M. Williams, 2005, pp. 1–18). Third, these appeals seem completely uninterested in these thinkers' own *self-understandings* or their surrounding thought-worlds (Schmidt, 1998, pp. 15–42). The fact that neither Thucydides nor Hobbes, for instance, was a self-conscious contributor to the realist tradition does not seem to matter for their purported membership within it.

Beyond these interpretive worries, to which I will return below, we might also ask another set of questions of any exercise of tradition-building: What purposes does it serve? What work is the tradition doing for its builders? In IR, for instance, one of the purposes served by appeals to a realist tradition is legitimation, 'confirming the continuing validity of "Realist" principles throughout history, and appropriating the authority of classical figures in political theory in their support' (M. Williams, 2005, p. 3). What work are appeals to a realist tradition doing in contemporary political theory?

I want to suggest that these appeals are performing at least three sorts of tasks. First, appeals to tradition do *boundary work*. That is, they help to demarcate the contours of the realist approach by identifying its 'unique and essential characteristics' and distinguishing it from other approaches (Gieryn, 1983; see also Bell, 2014). This boundary work has both an external and an internal dimension. The external dimension appeals to the idea of a tradition and canon in order to distinguish the realist approach from competitors and invest it with a certain intellectual authority. For instance, Raymond Geuss suggests that the realist approach develops a Hobbesian insight from the dawn of 'modern political philosophy' in Europe – that coordination 'is always a social achievement, and it is something attained and preserved, and generally achieved only at a certain price' (Geuss, 2008, p. 22). Geuss contrasts this realist tradition with an 'ethics-first' approach that traces its modern roots back to Kant, treats politics as applied ethics, and therefore privileges the demands of justice over those of political order. Those who want to 'develop the realistic spirit of Hobbes in the contemporary world' must take their bearings instead from Lenin, Nietzsche, and Weber. For Geuss, the neo-Kantian, 'ethics-first' approach of contemporary high liberals serves as the foil against which the realist alternative comes into view. Appeals to a modern tradition of thought stretching back to Hobbes lends this alternative the suggestion of some positive content and an apparent coherence that connects figures as diverse as Weber and Lenin.

Similarly, Matt Sleat appeals to a realist tradition to bring coherence to 'the work of a diverse range of political theorists' who do not always self-identify as realists. Assuming a pre-constituted 'realist tradition,' Sleat suggests that one of the things that links this diverse body of contemporary work is the common appeal 'to the key theorists in the realist canon, Thucydides, Machiavelli, Hobbes, Hume, Nietzsche, Weber, and Schmitt most notably.' Here, appeals to the 'realist canon' serve as markers of a common underlying set of commitments in a 'body of disparate and often disconnected work' (2013, p. 2). On Sleat's account (and that of others), these commitments center on a particular understanding of the political that serves not only to lend coherence to the realist approach but also to distinguish it more clearly from its high liberal targets.[8]

The internal dimension of this boundary work involves the division of the realist tradition itself and often serves to distinguish a preferred and acceptable version of realism from an impoverished alternative.[9] In this vein, Karuna Mantena distinguishes a 'moderating realism,' which traces its roots back to Thucydides, Hobbes, Montesquieu, Hume, Madison, and Burke and aims to contain and calm the 'passions, vices, and enthusiasms that drive political conflict and competition,' from a 'Machiavellian realism' that 'reaches its denouement in the defense of power politics' and amounts to 'a kind of idealization of the efficacy of political power' (2012, p. 455; see also, in a similar vein, Schlosser 2014, p. 242). The recent revival of realism in contemporary political theory is, Mantena suggests, much more in keeping with this 'moderating' strain. Here, the internal division of the realist tradition serves to contain its more normatively troubling elements and insulate the 'new realism' of contemporary political theory from these unwanted associations.

Geuss is also at pains to distinguish his own brand of realism from what he takes to be the 'conservative' and 'hard-edged' *Realpolitik* that he associates with IR realists like Hans Morgenthau (Geuss, 2001, p. 55, Geuss, 2010). It is not difficult to see why this kind of internal boundary work is seen to be necessary. Many of the most powerful critiques of realism have tended to reduce it to *Realpolitik* and to accuse it, accordingly, of casual skepticism and amoralism (Cohen, 1984; Beitz, 1999). Internal boundary work contains these criticisms by conceding their force against a particular strain of realism while resisting the suggestion that the strain exhausts the family of realist approaches.

Second, appeals to tradition perform *recovery work*. Here, a pre-constituted but neglected canon of realist texts serves as a resource through which to reclaim and recuperate a particular approach to political theorizing. This work is often underpinned by a narrative of decline – the capture of contemporary political theory and philosophy by 'high liberalism' or 'ideal theory' and a vision of politics centered on agreement, consent and harmony. Looking to the realist tradition and drawing from its canon of classic texts, one finds models for different ways of doing political theory. For instance, William Galston finds in thinkers like Machiavelli, Montesquieu, and Madison models for the kind of institutionally sensitive political theorizing that some contemporary realists advocate – a kind of political theorizing that treats institutions as something more than simply a 'means to the realization of antecedently established principles and aims' (2010, p. 393). If, as Galston suggests, the contemporary realists' 'preferred future resembles the political theory of an earlier period of modernity, and of classical antiquity as well,' then the realist tradition serves as a repository of exemplars for an approach to political theorizing that has been lost or forgotten (2010, p. 394).

For some, this project of recovery should also include the IR and 'Realpolitik' realism which Geuss, Mantena, and others seem so eager to quarantine. William Scheuerman, for instance, argues that mid-century thinkers like E.H. Carr, Hans Morgenthau, Reinhold Niebuhr, and Raymond Aron share 'canonical' forerunners, critical targets, and intellectual commitments with 'new realists' like Geuss and Williams (Scheuerman, 2013; Sleat, 2013). Turning back to this group of thinkers would help contemporary realists avoid reproducing the 'conceptual ambiguities' of their mid-century forerunners. It would also provide powerful examples of thinkers able to move beyond polemical critiques and toward 'a powerful descriptive account of real-life international politics'

(Scheuerman, 2013, p. 799). Attention to the tradition, on this view, can provide epistemic resources that may otherwise go untapped.[10]

Finally, appeals to tradition do *legitimating work*. In a quite straightforward sense, appeals to a realist tradition allow contemporary realists to resist the claim that their approach is entirely new, or worse, merely 'fashionable' (Finlayson, 2015). In this vein, Enzo Rossi and Matt Sleat argue:

> There is little completely new about contemporary realism if viewed as part of a tradition of thought that goes back at least to Thucydides … and continues through Augustine, Machiavelli, Hobbes, Hume, Nietzsche, Schmitt and Weber … Contemporary realism might look new to a discipline in which the application of Kantian ethics … has been so dominant for some four decades, along with other forms of moralism … But contemporary realism is thoroughly continuous with both the realist tradition generally and some of the specific concerns of IR realism (and, indeed, legal realism) (Rossi & Sleat, 2014, p. 697).

Here, a canon of classic works serves as a sign of historical continuity – a way to 'legitimize change by minimizing it' (Nardin, 1992, p. 7). On this account, realist approaches to political theory are hardly 'new' (Honig & Stears, 2011) and are certainly not fashionable (Rossi & Sleat, 2014, p. 691). They are part of an established and complex tradition of political thought that ought to be acknowledged and affirmed by its contemporary inheritors.

But claims about the old and enduring nature of the realist tradition also do a more complex form of legitimating work. Despite their sensitivity to local and temporal context, most self-identified political realists tend to assume that there are certain enduring and inescapable truths about politics – the ineradicability of conflict, the fragility of political order, and the persistence of 'power, powerlessness, cruelty, and fear' (Hawthorn, 2005, p. xi, see also Geuss, 2008, pp. 96–97). The assertion, then, 'that there is a Realist tradition' that stretches back to Thucydides 'is a key component of claims about the continuing salience and wisdom of Realism itself' (M. Williams, 2005, p. 3). If the Peloponnesian War was able to prompt a 'realist' analysis as readily as the cold war or if the English Civil War could illuminate the priority of political order as readily as contemporary Somalia, then realism's insistence that there are certain enduring facts about the political world seems all the more warranted. Recurrence, on this view, suggests correctness.

## 3. Contextualism and the tradition-building worry

Political realists' appeals to tradition are subject to the same criticisms lodged at their IR cousins: abstraction, selectiveness, and a lack of interest in thinkers' self-understandings. This is somewhat puzzling, given that contemporary realists in political theory profess a deep commitment to contextualism that their IR counterparts did not. That is, contemporary realists in political theory are committed to approaching both political actors and political thinkers as historically situated agents who are responding to and constrained by the social, institutional, and intellectual contexts of their times (B. Williams, 2005 ; Geuss, 2008; Rossi & Sleat, 2014). Within political theory, contextualist commitments of this sort have underpinned some of the most of formidable critiques of tradition-building (Skinner, 1969).

Contextualism is connected to at least three interrelated sets of commitments that contemporary self-proclaimed realists embrace, all of which are underpinned by a typically realist anti-moralism and anti-universalism. First, at a practical and prudential level, contextualism urges realists attempting to effect political change to be sensitive to endogenous, local complaints (Pettit, 2015). Prescriptions that are contextually sensitive in this way will have a better chance of success (Geuss, 2008, p. 8). Second, at a critical level, contextualism commits realists to the work of using historical and genealogical analysis to defamiliarize concepts and institutions that seem 'so natural and indispensable that one could not imagine a society that might lack [them]' (Geuss, 2008, p. 67). This critical contextualism connects to practical contextualism by diagnosing instances in which those offering prescriptions may be mistaking their own moral and political values for transcendent ones.

Third, at a methodological level, contextualism requires that realists reject (or at least a be skeptical toward) 'highly abstractive methods in political philosophy' (Geuss, 2005, p. 38) that aim at 'overarching algorithmic moral principles' that can be applied in any possible political circumstances (Rossi & Sleat, 2014, p. 694; see also B. Williams, 2005 , pp. 1–3). Critical contextualism aims at least in part to keep these methodological temptations toward abstraction and generalization at bay. Geuss (2008, p. 14) acknowledges, for instance, that humans in all times and places are constrained by the common desire for survival and nourishment, but doubts that the mild universal constraints entailed by such facts are very useful for political theory. When it comes to interesting questions, context and circumstance are crucial.

Turning from political practice and normative theory to the history of political thought, contextualism demands treating historical texts not as abstract philosophical arguments handed down for all time, but as works that attempt to respond to but are also constrained by the political, conceptual, and linguistic possibilities of their times. Even more strongly, these arguments were intended as polemical interventions in timely debates. The claims of historical thinkers 'are never above the battle; they are always part of the battle' (Skinner, 2008, p. xv, Skinner, 1969).

This aspect of contextualism poses the sharpest challenge to contemporary tradition-building realists. Skinner's early work draws on R.G. Collingwood's philosophy of history to deny the existence of permanent philosophical questions: 'what is thought to be permanent problem P is really a number of transitory problems $p_1$, $p_2$, $p_3$ ... whose individual peculiarities are blurred by the historical myopia of the person who lumps them together under the one name P' (Collingwood, 1939, p. 69). Following Collingwood, Skinner argues that the questions with which political thinkers are concerned transform themselves in subtle ways over time. There are, as Geuss puts it rather starkly, 'no interesting "eternal questions" of political philosophy' (2008, p. 13). Tradition-building realists commit a serious error, then, in suggesting that there is such a thing as a 'realist doctrine' or a 'realist tradition.' Beyond failing to recognize the subtle but significant transformation of questions over time, the commitment to the reality of doctrines and traditions is problematic because it is based on a potentially unwarranted assumption that an 'author must have had some doctrine, or a "message," which can be readily abstracted and more simply put' (Skinner, 1966, p. 209). The assumption is unwarranted, on Skinner's view, because political thought is difficult and often leads to confusion and changes of mind. The result of this thinking is often a series of 'scattered or quite incidental remarks' (Skinner, 1969, p. 7).

Faced with such scattered remarks, the doctrine-hunting or tradition-building interpreter is vulnerable to at least two kinds of error. First, she may be susceptible to a combination of *confirmation and selection bias*. She may, consciously or not, find only those ideas in a thinker's work that confirm his identification with the relevant doctrine or tradition. For example, if an interpreter approaches John Locke as the originator of a liberal doctrine of government by consent, she may be inclined to attend only to those portions of the *Second Treatise* (e.g. the account of the contractual origins of government) that affirm this account, while failing to attend to those that do not (Skinner, 1969). Similarly, if an interpreter approaches Thucydides as the originator of a realist tradition, she may be inclined to attend only to those portions of the *History* (e.g. the Melian Dialog, the account of the civil war in Corcyra) that affirm this account, while failing to attend to those that do not. Second, she may impose a *false sense of coherence* on the texts she is reading. Looking for evidence of a doctrine or membership in a tradition, the interpreter may slide almost imperceptibly into the project of 'constructing doctrines more abstract than any which the writer in question might seem to have held, in order to dispose of inconsistencies in his opinions which would otherwise remain' (Skinner, 1966, p. 210). The result of such an interpretive project is 'a history of thought which no one ever actually succeeded in thinking, at a level of coherence which no one ever actually attained' (Skinner, 1969, p. 18).

To my mind, these methodological concerns are at least somewhat overstated. There do seem to be basic normative questions that recur, admittedly in somewhat different articulations and from various points of view, through time.[11] They include: What is the best regime? Who should rule? Under what conditions is political power legitimate? And, especially important for realists: What is the relative primacy of justice and political order? While the political concepts deployed in these questions, the range of possible answers, and the criteria for evaluating plausible answers have undoubtedly varied across time and space, both the questions and the answers – even when understood in their full contextual richness – retain a certain transhistorical coherence that renders plausible the portrait of an ongoing (though often not self-conscious) conversation. In fact, if his repeated references to a republican (or neo-Roman) 'tradition' are anything to go by, Skinner himself seems to have warmed to something like this view (1998, 2008).

Let us assume, then, that only a more moderate version of these contextualist worries is right. Contemporary realist invocations a 'tradition' still seem to run into trouble. They may be insufficiently attuned to the ways in which concepts and commitments change subtly over time. They may be likely to take a small selection of a work as both representative of a thinker's view and as sufficient evidence for his membership in the realist tradition. Or, they may impose a false sense of coherence on a thinker's work and thereby offer a reconstruction of his arguments that the thinker himself could neither recognize nor affirm.

Realists might respond in two ways. First, they might suggest that these worries do not bear directly on the kind of work most contemporary realists see themselves as doing when they appeal to a realist tradition. Political realists probably see themselves as appealing to what John Gunnell (1987, pp. 85–90) calls an analytical, rather than a historical tradition (Gunnell, 1987, pp. 85–90) – a set of structural and conceptual similarities among arguments, texts, and ideas rather than a history of actual discourse or conscious continuity. Unlike a historical tradition, an analytical tradition is a self-consciously and 'retrospectively created construct determined by present criteria and concerns' (Schmidt, 1998, p. 25).[12] While an analytical tradition may deploy a chronological account of intellectual history, such accounts are akin to the 'philosopher's schematic version of speculative history' (Rawls, 2007, p. 11) – narratives about how particular sets of ideas or arguments *could* plausibly have arisen. Such narratives do not quite require 'setting aside all the facts' (Rousseau, 1997, p. 132), but they do abstract from such facts in order to better understand processes of conceptual development. If the 'tradition' to which contemporary realists appeal is an analytical one, it is not clear why the contextualist worries outlined above should concern them. More specifically, if what realists are doing when they appeal to a 'realist tradition' is flagging conceptual and structural similarities among ideas and arguments, why should conceptual change, selection bias, or false coherence count as problems?

However, it is not at all clear that the traditions to which most political realists appeal are in fact meant as wholly analytical. The invocations of tradition surveyed in the previous section suggest that many contemporary realists have, at a minimum, mistaken an analytical tradition for a historical one. For Gunnell, this is the familiar trap into which canon builders predictably fall. They reify 'an analytical construct' and represent 'what is in fact a retrospectively and externally demarcated tradition as an actual or self-constituted tradition' (Gunnell, 1986, p. 95; see similarly Gunnell, 1987; Schmidt, 1998). More importantly, though, if political realists were merely appealing to an analytical tradition, this appeal could not do the work that they want it to do. This is certainly true in cases where such appeals do legitimating work. Here, references to a pre-constituted, historically continuous, and ancient tradition are essential to resisting efforts to class realism as 'new' or 'fashionable.' By its very nature, legitimating work seems to depend on the power and authority of an appeal to a *historical* tradition.

This seems less clear in cases of boundary and recovery work, whose intrinsic logic does not seem to require robust claims about the historical reality of a given tradition. One could imagine boundary work that proceeds on overtly analytical grounds (e.g. work that considers whether a given argument shares some number of core commitments that are seen as necessary and/or sufficient for membership in a given tradition). Similarly, one could imagine recovery work that proceeds along similarly analytical lines (e.g. work that looks to historical thinkers for concepts and arguments that are both consistent with and analytically useful for contemporary work in a given tradition). However, as we have seen, efforts at boundary and recovery work in the literature on realism do not tend to proceed in these ways, but rather assume a pre-constituted historical tradition whose bounds and membership have already been settled.

Realists' second response to contextualist critiques might be to wonder why, beyond the embarrassment of conceptual confusion, contemporary realists should care about these worries. One might concede that efforts at tradition-building are inconsistent with realism's contextualist commitments but still insist that this inconsistency has little bearing on the core work of contemporary realists – articulating a coherent critique of (and perhaps even an alternative to) contemporary liberal political philosophy. I think realists still have good reason to accept contextualist worries about tradition building. A disregard of context can prevent us from learning what past thinkers might teach us. To take an example from my own work, when he eventually confronts the possibility of nuclear annihilation, Hans Morgenthau abandons many of his earlier realist commitments and comes to envision the possibility of a world state with a monopoly on nuclear violence (Craig, 2003; Scheuerman, 2009, 2011). On my reading, he also embraces an ambitious formative project that aims to cultivate the salutary fear of nuclear death that he thinks is required to get us to accept our common humanity and subject ourselves to a world state. This transformation in his thought, I suggest, tells us something about the limits of his realist commitments in the face of the radical novelty of nuclear weapons (McQueen, 2016b). If one approached Morgenthau merely with the goal of identifying precursors and examples of arguments that match one's conception of realism, one might miss what he can tell us about the limits of realism or the difficulty of being a thoroughgoing realist. Surely these are things that contemporary realists should want to know.

## 4. Toward a realist tradition

Should contemporary realists abandon the idea of a realist tradition altogether? No such a drastic remedy seems necessary. Here I propose a set of inclusion criteria through which we might construct a realist tradition that is consistent with moderate contextualist commitments but still allows us to group similar arguments together for analytical purposes. The discussion above implies that such criteria must do three things.

First, they must preserve the analytical value of the idea of a tradition. Our inclusion criteria should be capable of producing an account of the tradition that captures some of the structural and functional similarities among the arguments of contemporary realists and those whom they identify as their intellectual forerunners.

Second, our criteria must be capable of giving us an account of the tradition that is consistent with at least a moderate version of the contextualism that most realists profess. That is, our criteria must be sensitive to the problems of selection and confirmation bias outlined above, as well as to the self-understandings and thought-worlds of historical thinkers. Many of these thinkers did not affirm a 'realist doctrine' or see themselves as 'realists.' Given the conceptual and argumentative resources available to them, one might reasonably doubt whether they even could have.[13]

Third, our criteria should be capable of producing an account of the realist tradition that is at least somewhat comprehensive and captures a plurality of understandings of realism. That is, it should be open to the ways in which these understandings have, over time, appeared, changed, come under pressure, and clashed. Our criteria should be sensitive to the fact that realism has been a changing and contested tradition, the product of self-conscious tradition-building by scholars with their own intellectual agendas (Bell, 2014). However, our criteria and the resulting conception of the realist tradition should not bow unduly to these scholarly agendas. While the conception should capture a plurality of understandings of realism, it should not do so in a way that imports boundary, recovery, and legitimacy work *as a matter of definition*.

Bell (2014) has recently proposed a 'comprehensive' definition of the liberal tradition that is intended to respond to similar worries. Adapting this conception for the realist case would give us something like this: the realist tradition is constituted by *the range of arguments that have been classified as realist, and recognized as such by self-proclaimed realists, across time and space*.[14] This comprehensive definition of a tradition allows for inclusion criteria that fulfill the terms just mentioned. First, it offers us a set of inclusion criteria that preserves the analytical and classificatory value of the idea of a tradition of thought. Second, it does this in a way that is sensitive to context. Just as Bell's discussion of the liberal tradition allows for a clear distinction between liberal thinkers and liberal arguments, a similar discussion of realism pushes us to attend to the distinction between realist arguments and the classification of thinkers themselves as 'realists.' For instance, the comprehensive conception allows us to retroactively classify some of Machiavelli's *arguments* about the autonomy of politics and Hobbes' arguments about the priority of political order as realist without falling into the anachronistic trap of identifying these thinkers themselves as 'realists' or of implicitly attributing to them the intention of putting forward a 'realist doctrine.' If we can successfully avoid this problem, we may then be more prepared to recognize the places in which these thinkers abandon or revise their realist arguments. This recognition, I suggest, makes it more likely that we will be able to learn something important about the limits of realism and the difficulties of remaining a thoroughgoing realist. This is, as suggested above, surely information that contemporary realists should want to have. However, this contextual sensitivity still allows the comprehensive conception to take the analytical tradition-building attempts of contemporary self-proclaimed realists seriously. It does not allow contextualist worries to override the considered views of these contemporary realists about the kinds of historical arguments that have shaped their own commitments.

Third, the comprehensive conception offers a set of inclusion criteria that are capable of producing an account of the realist tradition that will not be entirely beholden to the particular understandings of realism and the realist tradition that have commanded such attention in recent years. However, this comprehensive conception would not produce an implausibly expansive account of the realist tradition either. As Bell suggests, the recognition condition imposes an epistemic limit: 'only those positions *affirmed* at some point in time by groups of *self-proclaimed* [realists] should be included' (2014, p. 690). The implicit but reasonable assumption here seems to be that, while contemporary self-proclaimed realists may have all sorts of presentist purposes in mind when they return to the work of an historical thinker, they are still, on balance, those best suited to recognize realist concepts and arguments when they see them. The requirement that multiple self-proclaimed realists would have to affirm the position offers some protection against individual idiosyncrasies. Of course, this condition also raises a threshold question. How many self-proclaimed realists over how wide a span of time must identify an argument as realist for it to be included in our account of the tradition? Bell defends the following temporal threshold in the case of the liberal tradition:

> [T]o stake a claim for inclusion there must be sustained usage by numerous prominent ideological entrepreneurs over at least two generations. Otherwise, the bar for inclusion is set too low. That H.G. Wells declared himself a 'liberal fascist' is nowhere near enough to warrant incorporating fascism into the liberal tradition, for barely anyone else followed him along that idiosyncratic path. But … 'libertarianism' clearly meets the entry criteria. So too do the social democratic arguments scorned by libertarians (2014, p. 690).

Whether this specific threshold is appropriate in the realist case (or for that matter, the liberal one) is not something I am prepared to evaluate here. However, it is worth noting that a comprehensive conception with a two-generation temporal threshold would put pressure on existing accounts of the realist tradition in at least two directions. First, it would prompt us to consider for inclusion those arguments identified as realist by self-proclaimed realists in postwar International Relations. These are precisely the 'hard-edged' and 'Realpolitik' arguments that the boundary-work by Geuss, Mantena, and others would have us quarantine or exclude. The arguments of thinkers like Reinhold Niebuhr, E.H. Carr, Hans Morgenthau, George Kennan, and Kenneth Waltz would be included on these criteria. Second, a comprehensive conception would prompt us to be alert to the possibility of a more global account of the realist tradition. Not only are there contemporary self-proclaimed realists working outside of Western academia, but there are also a number of arguments by non-Western thinkers (e.g. Kautilya) that have been repeatedly identified as realist by self-proclaimed realists in the West.[15] Thus, while a comprehensive conception sets inclusion limits that guard against an implausibly expansive account of the realist tradition, it is also open to the possibility that realist arguments may be found beyond the familiar reaches of Western intellectual history.

## 5. Conclusion

To sum up, appeals to 'tradition' may well be the product of political realism's recent arrival to debates in contemporary political theory. In the absence of any firm agreement on the nature of the realist project or on realism's core commitments, its proponents have tended to agree on its intellectual lineage. This account of the realist tradition has performed three kinds of work that may seem especially important to those defending a new and emergent approach – boundary, recovery, and legitimating work. However, these appeals to a realist tradition rest uneasily with realism's contextualist commitments and come with epistemic costs.

Does this mean that realists should give up on the idea of a tradition altogether? I have suggested that this would be too hasty. By taking a comprehensive conception of their tradition, realists can preserve its analytical value whilst avoiding the most serious contextualist critiques. Doing so would require giving up on the forms of boundary, recovery, and legitimating work that assume a pre-constituted tradition with stable bounds and membership. It would require approaching the realist tradition with the aim of *discovering*, rather than confirming, realism's core commitments. My intuition, which obviously awaits future vindication, is that the account of the realist tradition that would emerge from these inclusion criteria would resemble the provisional one that I offered at the outset. Regardless, this article has suggested one way in which realism's project of tradition-building might proceed on firmer footing.

## Notes

1. McQueen (in press) stresses the second observation and argues that the classical IR theorists belong in the political realist 'tradition' on conceptual grounds.
2. This conceptualization builds on B. Williams (2005, pp. 1–17), Geuss (2008, pp. 1–18), Galston (2010, pp. 385–387), Mantena (2012, p. 455), Rossi and Sleat (2014, pp. 689–691). McQueen (2016a) offers this conceptualization and McQueen (in press) examines these commitments in more detail.
3. I owe this conception of a 'distinctive family' to Joshua Cohen.
4. For this reason, it would be extremely difficult (perhaps impossible) to establish necessary and sufficient conditions for an approach being 'realist.' Drawing on the social science literature on concept formation (which takes its bearings from Wittgenstein), we might instead use the family resemblance approach (Goertz, 2005, p. 7; see also Bell, 2009, p. 3).
5. For instance, realism would rule out a 'republicanism' whose institutional proposals depended on severe and virtuous civic self-abnegation or agreement about the common good, but not one that stressed institutional checks and contestation (Pettit, 2015).
6. For various ways of carving up the intellectual space, see: Donelan (1993), Wight (1991), Nardin (1992), Boucher (1998). For a critical analysis of the place of tradition in IR, see Jeffrey (2005).
7. The discussion below draws on Bell's (2009, p. 6) notion of an 'expansive tradition' as well as his description of the problems of abstraction, selectiveness, and self-understanding.
8. Resisting an account of realism as kind of non-ideal critique of ideal theory (Valentini, 2012), Sleat argues: 'If we think about the canon of realist thinkers in political theory … then it is not easy to see exactly how they count as realists if by "realism" we mean a concern for the implementation of ideals in practice or the need to engage in more fact-sensitive normative theorizing.' While non-ideal critiques of ideal theory still operate well within the ambit of liberal theory, no 'canonical' realists, 'apart from Hume (and possibly Hobbes under certain interpretations), can plausibly be thought of as liberal theorists … Realism stands to liberalism as a fundamentally different conception of politics – one which has very distinct notions regarding the purpose and limits of politics, as well as the appropriate ambitions of political theory' (Sleat, 2014, pp. 4–5). These kinds of appeals to a 'realist tradition' seem to assume precisely what is in question – the content and coherence of 'realism' itself.
9. This kind of boundary work is analogous to the attempts of some within the liberal tradition to distinguish classical liberalism (or libertarianism) from social liberalism (Bell, 2014).
10. For another argument in this vein, though one that proceeds along more conceptual lines, see McQueen (in press).
11. For an attempt to carve out a more modest version of the Collingwoodian claim about perennial problems, see: Rawls (2007, pp. 103–104).
12. One might argue that 'analytical tradition' involves oxymoron, since tradition simply entails a social process of actual transmission (Condren, 1997, p. 48). Granting the point for argument's sake, one might simply substitute a different term.
13. Compare Bell's (2014, p. 688) claim that Locke lacked access the 'range of concepts and arguments' that would have made it possible for him to be, in any interesting sense, a 'liberal.'

14. Bell's original definition is: 'the liberal tradition is constituted by *the sum of the arguments that have been classified as liberal, and recognized as such by other self-proclaimed liberals, across time and space*' (2014, pp. 689–690). For reasons I lack time to discuss here, I do not find Bell's discussion of a 'summative' tradition fully appropriate for current purposes. I have therefore substituted 'range' for Bell's 'sum' as well.
15. On the first point, realist arguments and concepts have a robust presence among scholars of International Relations and policy-makers in China (Wang, 2009; Schneider, 2014; Lynch, 2015, pp. 155–238). On the second point, Morgenthau, for instance, repeatedly invokes the classical Indian thinker Kautilya's arguments in a realist vein in *Politics Among Nations* (Morgenthau, 1954).

## Acknowledgements

This paper was greatly improved in response to comments from Burke Hendrix, Terry Nardin, Philip Pettit, Andy Sabl, Rahul Sagar, Matt Sleat, other participants at a 2015 workshop on realism at National University of Singapore, and an anonymous reviewer.

## Disclosure statement

No potential conflict of interest was reported by the author.

## References

Beitz, C. R. (1999). *Political theory and International Relations* (2nd ed.). Princeton, NJ: Princeton University Press.
Bell, D. (2009). Introduction: Under an empty sky-realism and political thoery. In D. Bell (Ed.), *Political thought and international relations: Variations on a realist theme* (pp. 1–25). Cambridge: Cambridge University Press.
Bell, D. (2014). What is liberalism? *Political theory, 42*, 682–715.
Boucher, D. (1998). *Political theories of international relations: From thucydides to the present*. Oxford: Oxford University Press.
Brown, C., Nardin, T., & Rengger, N. (Eds.). (2002). *International relations in political thought: Texts from the ancient Greeks to the first world war*. Cambridge: Cambridge University Press.
Cohen, M. (1984). Moral skepticism and international relations. *Philosophy and Public Affairs, 13*, 299–346.
Collingwood, R. G. (1939). *An autobiography*. Oxford: Oxford University Press.

Condren, C. (1997). Political theory and the problem of anachronism. In A. Vincent (Ed.), *Political theory: Tradition and diversity* (pp. 45–66). Cambridge: Cambridge University Press.

Craig, C. (2003). *Glimmer of a New Leviathan: Total war in the realism of Niebuhr, Morgenthau, and Waltz*. New York, NY: Columbia University Press.

Donelan, M. (1993). *Elements of international political theory*. Oxford: Oxford University Press.

Finlayson, L. (2015). With radicals like these, who needs conservatives? Doom, gloom, and realism in political theory. *European Journal of Political Theory*. Early view. Retrieved December 16, 2015, from http://ept.sagepub.com/content/early/2015/01/30/1474885114568815

Galston, W. A. (2010). Realism in political theory. *European Journal of Political Theory, 9*, 385–411.

Geuss, R. (2001). *History and illusion in politics*. Cambridge: Cambridge University Press.

Geuss, R. (2005). *Outside ethics*. Princeton, NJ: Princeton University Press.

Geuss, R. (2008). *Philosophy and real politics*. Princeton, NJ: Princeton University Press.

Geuss, R. (2010). *Politics and the imagination*. Princeton, N.J: Princeton University Press.

Gieryn, T. F. (1983). Boundary-work and the demarcation of science from non-science: strains and interests in professional ideologies of scientists. *American Sociological Review, 48*, 781–795.

Goertz, G. (2005). *Social science concepts: A user's guide*. Princeton, NJ: Princeton University Press.

Gray, J. (1995). *Enlightenment's wake: Politics and culture at the close of the modern age*. London: Routledge.

Gray, J. (2000). *Two faces of liberalism* (1st ed.). New York, NY: New Press.

Gunnell, J. G. (1986). *Between philosophy and politics: The alienation of political theory*. Amherst, MA: University of Massachusetts Press.

Gunnell, J. G. (1987). *Political theory: Tradition and interpretation*. Lanham, MD: University Press of America.

Hawthorn, G. (2005). Introduction. In G. Hawthorn (Ed.), *In the beginning was the deed* (pp. xi–xx). Princeton, NJ: Princeton University Press.

Honig, B. (1993). *Political theory and the displacement of politics*. Ithaca, NY: Cornell University Press.

Honig, B., & Stears, M. (2011). The new realism: From modus vivendi to justice. In J. Floyd & M. Stears (Eds.), *Political philosophy versus history? Contextualism and real politics in contemporary political thought* (pp. 177–205). Cambridge: Cambridge University Press.

Jeffrey, R. (2005). Tradition as invention: The 'traditions tradition' and the history of ideas in international relations. *Millennium: Journal of International Studies, 34*, 57–84.

Lynch, D. (2015). *China's futures: PRC elites debate economics, politics, and foreign policy*. Stanford, CA: Stanford University Press.

Mantena, K. (2012). Another realism: The politics of gandhian nonviolence. *American Political Science Review, 106*, 455–470.

McQueen, A. (2016a). Political realism and moral corruption. *European Journal of Political Theory*. Early view. Retrieved October 1, 2016, from http://ept.sagepub.com/content/early/2015/01/30/1474885114568815

McQueen, A. (2016b). *Political realism in apocalyptic times*. Unpublished manuscript.

McQueen, A. (in press). The case for kinship: Political realism and classical realism. In M. Sleat (Ed.), *Politics recovered: Essays on realist political thought* (chapter 10). New York, NY: Columbia University Press.

Morgenthau, H. J. (1946). *Scientific man vs. power politics*. Chicago: University of Chicago Press.

Morgenthau, H. J. (1954). *Politics among nations: The struggle for power and peace* (2nd ed.). New York: Albert A. Knopf.

Murray, A. J. H. (1997). *Reconstructing realism*. Edinburgh: Edinburgh University Press.

Nardin, T. (1992). Ethical traditions in international affairs. In T. Nardin & D. R. Mapel (Eds.), *Traditions of international ethics* (pp. 1–22). Cambridge: Cambridge University Press.

Pettit, P. (2015). Political realism meets civic republicanism. *Critical Review of International Social and Political Philosophy*. doi:http://dx.doi.org/10.1080/13698230.2017.1293912

Rawls, J. (2001). *Justice as fairness: A restatement*. Cambridge, MA: Harvard University Press.

Rawls, J. (2007). *Lectures on the history of political philosophy*. Cambridge, MA: Belknap Press.

Rossi, E., & Sleat, M. (2014). Realism in normative political theory. *Philosophy Compass, 9*, 689–701.

Rousseau, J.-J. (1997). Discourse on the origin and the foundations of inequality among men. In V. Gourevitch (Ed.), *The discourses and other early political writings* (pp. 113–222). Cambridge: Cambridge University Press.

Scheuerman, W. E. (2009). *Hans Morgenthau: Realism and beyond*. Cambridge: Polity Press.

Scheuerman, W. E. (2011). *The realist case for global reform*. Cambridge: Polity Press.

Scheuerman, W. E. (2013). The realist revival in political philosophy, or: Why new is not always improved. *International Politics, 50*, 798–814.

Schlosser, J. A. (2014). Herodotean realism. *Political Theory, 42*, 239–261.

Schmidt, B. C. (1998). *The political discourse of anarchy: A disciplinary history of international relations*. Albany, NY: State University of New York Press.

Schneider, F. (2014). Reconceptualising world order: Chinese political thought and its challenge to International Relations theory. *Review of International Studies, 40*, 683–703.

Sigwart, H.-J. (2013). The logic of legitimacy: Ethics in political realism. *The Review of Politics, 75*, 407–432.

Skinner, Q. (1966). The limits of historical explanations. *Philosophy, 41*, 199–215.

Skinner, Q. (1969). Meaning and understanding in the history of ideas. *History and Theory, 8*, 3–53.

Skinner, Q. (1998). *Liberty before liberalism*. Cambridge: Cambridge University Press. Retrieved from December 17, 2015, from http://www.cambridge.org/us/academic/subjects/history/history-ideas-and-intellectual-history/liberty-liberalism-1

Skinner, Q. (2008). *Hobbes and republican liberty*. Cambridge: Cambridge University Press.

Sleat, M. (2013). *Liberal realism: A realist theory of liberal politics*. Manchester, NH: Manchester University Press.

Sleat, M. (2014). Realism, liberalism and non-ideal theory or, are there two ways to do realistic political theory? *Political Studies, 64*, 27–41.

Valentini, L. (2012). Ideal vs. non-ideal theory: A conceptual map. *Philosophy Compass, 7*, 654–664.

Wang, Y. (2009). China: Between copying and constructing. In A. B. Tickner & O. Weaver (Eds.), *International Relations scholarship around the world* (pp. 103–119). Abingdon: Routledge.

Wight, M. (1960). Why is there no international theory? *International Relations, 2*, 35–48.

Wight, M. (1991). *International theory: The three traditions*. G. Wight & B. Porter (Eds.). London: Leicester Universtiy Press.

Williams, B. (2005). *In the beginning was the deed: Realism and moralism in political argument*. G. Hawthorn (Ed.). Princeton, NJ: Princeton University Press.

Williams, M. (2005). *The realist tradition and the limits of international relations*. Cambridge: Cambridge University Press.

# The new realism and the old

Terry Nardin

**ABSTRACT**
The tradition of political realism denies the relevance of morality to politics and asserts the value of prudence. The new realists in political theory repeat these claims in the context of criticising a style of political theorising they identify with Rawls and Kant. Some affirm the importance of experience and judgment, echoing an earlier generation of political theorists, including Oakeshott and Arendt. Others locate the distinctive character of politics in the problem of establishing order and legitimising it, and because they are moral sceptics they treat legitimacy as contextual and plural. But arguments about legitimacy must address the difference between governing people and dominating them. The new realists therefore find themselves encountering the question of justice, from which their tradition has tried without success to distance itself. To show that questions of order and justice are related, I briefly consider Kant's political thought. Like the new realists, Kant treats politics as distinct from ethics and looks for principles of legitimacy that are internal to political order. Instead of making Kant a target for criticism, the new realists could draw on his insights to strengthen their own account of the autonomy of politics. Doing so would also strengthen their case against the simplistic moralising of academic political philosophy and further illuminate the contribution of realism to political thought.

Ten years after the emergence of 'the new realism' as a movement in contemporary political theory, it is clear that its significance lies not in having formulated a coherent view of political ethics but in reminding theorists of questions that cannot be avoided in discussing the topic. Political realism implies rejecting political idealism, where idealism means being concerned with moral purposes to be pursued and moral principles to be respected in pursuing them. The most influential of the new realists – Bernard Williams and Raymond Geuss – focused their criticism on 'applied ethics' as an approach to moral philosophy and on the efforts of John Rawls, and philosophers influenced by or responding to him, to identify principles of justice for assessing the moral legitimacy of political regimes. But as those engaged in this critical enterprise are only slowly coming to appreciate, the distinction between idealism and realism is hard to sustain. Rawls, for example, was concerned not only to articulate ideals but also to explore what he called 'non-ideal theory'. And on the premise that what was wrong with Rawls-inspired thinking was its attachment to liberal principles, the new realists have looked for non-liberal sources of political legitimacy, hardly noticing that Rawls himself was doing something similar in his later work.

My aim in this paper is to unsettle the idealist-realist distinction on which realism depends and to do this by examining not Rawls but Kant, the arch-idealist identified by the new realists as inspiring Rawlsian liberalism. This identification is evident in references to Rawls's views as an expression of 'Kantian deontology'. But Kant can with equal logic be claimed for political realism since what has emerged in the new realist literature as the defining postulate of political realism, the autonomy of the political, distinguishes Kant's philosophy of politics from his moral philosophy. I do not wish to argue that Kant is a political realist, however, but rather to suggest that the ease with which the argument can be made reveals the vacuity of the expression 'political realism' as it is commonly used. The concerns now identified as realist in fact arise wherever politics is practiced and discussed. Unlike those who suggest that realism should be understood as 'a return to a more traditional way of doing political philosophy' (Rossi, 2016, p. 417) – which implies the existence of an agreed view of political philosophy that Rawlsian liberalism had ruptured – I argue that realist ideas can be found within the discourses the new realists set out to criticise.

## Some meanings of 'political realism'

A historian might identify several realist moments in modern political thought. One is the realism-idealism debate in international relations, beginning in the 1930s, about how to respond to Nazi and Soviet aggression, that pitted traditional policies like the balance of power against relying on international law and institutions (Herz, 1951). Another is the behavioural revolution in American political science, which imagined a science of politics in which political theory would be 'empirical' rather than normative. Earlier moments include Marx's criticisms of what he and Engels called the German ideology, Hegel's rejection of Kant's idea of a universal morality in favour of the embedded moral practices of actual communities, Machiavelli's suggestion that imagining an ideal polity is the surest road to ruin in governing, and the endless production of works on prudential statecraft throughout the modern period. The ascendance of political realism in political theory today can therefore be read as yet another 'Machiavellian moment' in the history of political thought (Pocock, 1975). Nor are the kinds of concerns identified in Western thought as realist limited to the West: there was in ancient India an interest in policies for achieving *artha* (economic prosperity or security) as an alternative to the practice of dharma (propriety and duty), and in China a tradition of *fa jia* (often translated as 'legalism' but perhaps better understood as a pragmatic approach to public administration) competing with Confucian ideals of virtue and right conduct. There is, then, a common and persistent tension between principles and prudence in governing, between a government's respecting its own laws and securing them against decay or destruction. The politics of realism, wherever it is practiced, is the politics of prudence, policy and pragmatic adjustment to circumstances.

There is, moreover, a connection between practical realism and realism in philosophy. Here the contrast is not with moral or political idealism but 'Idealism' understood as the philosophical argument that experience is mediated by thought and therefore by ideas. The things we call factual, true, or real are verdicts on what we experience: inferences based ultimately on sensation and perception, observation and measurement, judgment and interpretation. Philosophical realism is a response to this argument that truth is what is deemed to be true within a community of authoritative judges such as the scientific community. In the form this view took in the twentieth century, under the label 'poststructuralism', the claim was that meanings cannot be detached from conventions of thinking and speaking. Much as nineteenth-century German and British Idealists had argued that truth in science, history, or morals was determined by the canons of the relevant mode. Poststructuralists shared with Quine, Strawson, Putnam and other mainstream philosophers the view that truth rests on the coherence of statements within a particular universe of discourse. What is true and therefore real cannot be known except through conceptual frameworks that are plural and incommensurable. Philosophical realism denies these claims.

Words ending in '-ism' or '-ist' can be troublesome, however. The problem is that such words often identify outlooks that combine different and even contradictory arguments. Philosophy is about arguments and it requires making distinctions, not lumping things together. When we use those words we detach arguments from their contexts, thereby creating ambiguity and obscurity even when our motive is analytical rather than polemical. And though the contexts in which 'realism' and 'realist' are used can illuminate their intended meaning, caution is still needed when we use those words. Does 'realism' identify a consistent set of arguments or a discourse that admits of argumentative disagreement? Is political realism a theory or an ideology? Is it a kind of politics or a kind of political theorising? Such questions need to be answered before the words can be used philosophically. Like other political words, 'realism' is better treated as something to be investigated than as a tool of inquiry.

In casual speech, the word 'realism' identifies a disposition. To be realistic is to be judicious in applying rules and pragmatic in pursuing ends. It is to choose attainable goals and proportion one's effort without taking excessive risks. A realistic person 'accepts the existing framework for defining what is possible and impossible and tries to cut his desires to fit the cloth which his particular society has made available' (Geuss, 2015, p. 15). In this everyday sense of the term, being realistic in politics does not differ from being realistic in any other activity. The distinctive character of *political* realism emerges when attention is focused on the demands of acquiring, maintaining, and using power in a state. We may no longer speak of 'statecraft' and call its practitioners 'statesmen', but we cannot avoid making a distinction between matters of state and other matters, between realism generally and political realism. Here, the word 'realism' suggests a disposition that is especially appropriate to governing, and it implies some way of differentiating political activity from other kinds of activity. One way to do that is to argue that moral considerations should not have privileged status in making political decisions. Realism, on this view, is a cognitive claim, not an attitude or disposition.

The idea of realism in political *theory* introduces another layer of complexity related to the distinction between acting and theorising. At the level of action, there is realism (however defined) in the conduct of political affairs. At the level of theory, it is theorising itself that can be realist in some manner: empirical, scientific, critical, sceptical or however realist theorising is defined. The new realism in political theory is concerned with realist theorising as well as realist politics, sometimes without distinguishing between them. Such inattention to the boundaries between politics and political theory reflects the assumption, not limited to the new realism, that political theorising is inherently political because its aims are prescriptive rather than purely descriptive or explanatory.

Although the new realism presents itself as prescriptive, it has also given rise to a descriptive and explanatory literature. There are now many efforts to survey this literature, to identify its themes and to identify different kinds of realism. One observer, for example, distinguishes what she calls 'displacement realism', which criticises political theory for neglecting genuine politics by treating it as a branch of applied ethics rather than an arena for deliberative disagreement, from 'detachment realism', which criticises political theory for being too abstract and idealistic to provide adequate practical guidance (Baderin, 2014). The implication is either that political theorists should stand aside and let politics flourish on its own or that they should embrace practical politics by becoming less abstract and utopian. Another observer identifies as hallmarks of the new realism in political theory a concern with moral psychology, with the institutional context for political activity, and with the importance of compromise (Galston, 2010). More convincing than either of these portraits, however, is the suggestion that what ties new realist arguments together is a concern with 'the autonomy of the political' (Rossi & Sleat, 2014) – a suggestion to which I will return below.

To reject moralistic, idealistic or esoteric theorising is not necessarily to argue for a particular alternative. The new realism has been aptly characterised as 'an intellectual moment of resistance' rather than a unified school of thought with agreed aims or principles (Philp, 2012, p. 631). And it has been criticised for failing to provide a coherent alternative to prevailing theories (Galston, 2010, pp. 408–409). But that realists disagree does not mean that they cannot provide such an alternative. Williams in particular has tried to develop a substantive theory of politics on realist premises. The question is whether he or anyone else can come up with a theory that is either coherent or new.

## Two realist themes

In the new realist literature, then, different arguments are made under the banner of political realism. Instead of examining this literature to map its various concerns, I want to highlight two themes that justify its appropriating the name 'realism' because they are the themes of earlier realisms. The prominence of these themes in new realist discourse suggests that the main contribution of the new realism to political theory has been to revive themes temporarily eclipsed by other concerns.

In the past, those called political realists argued that prudence, not personal morality, should guide the decisions of leaders. To be a realist with respect to politics was either to reject morality as an illusion or to advocate *raison d'état* or *Realpolitik* as a style of governing, though often in ways more nuanced than these expressions now connote.

The first of these elements, moral scepticism, is a meta-ethical position. It may reject the possibility of genuine moral claims or suggest, more cautiously, that such claims cannot be firmly established. Moral sceptics sometimes accuse moralists of hypocrisy. The Athenian realists in the Melian dialogue dramatised by Thucydides, like Thrasymachus in Plato's *Republic*, dismiss talk of justice as rationalising the interests of the strong – a claim that reappears in the Marxist critique of ideology and, inverted, in Nietzsche's criticism of Christian morality as voicing the interests of the weak. Such 'sceptical realism' can range from cynicism about people's motives for making moral arguments to doubt that moral precepts, or at least abstract moralism, can provide an adequate guide to practice.

The new realism shares this traditional scepticism. Williams, for example, is critical of 'applied ethics', which seems to him to involve a crude casuistry scarcely deserving the title of moral philosophy. The chief defect of applied ethics is that its practitioners substitute principles for judgment: 'some people have a bit of ready-made philosophical theory, and they whiz in, a bit like hospital auxiliary personnel who aren't actually doctors' (Williams, 1983, p. 43). Or as he put it on another occasion, a person might 'acquire an excellent Ph.D. [in moral philosophy] and yet be someone whose judgement you would not trust on anything' (Williams, 2005, p. 46). The sort of casuistry he has in mind is illustrated by Peter Singer's argument that those living in rich countries are morally obligated to give away most of their wealth to relieve famine in poor countries (Singer, 1972). Williams is challenging the view that philosophers have skills as moralists that equip them for political activism. But he also wants to unsettle the conviction that morality – any morality – can provide demonstrable and therefore univocal answers to moral questions such that, having arrived at one of them, a person could judge or act without regret. These arguments, if sound, undermine the claim that moral values are the most important values a society can have. This does not mean that anti-moralism precludes having a theory of politics, but it does mean that such a theory must be more than a system of moral principles or utilitarian maxims.

Raymond Geuss also faults applied ethics as an approach to politics. He has two objections to what he calls political moralism, one having to do with the nature of politics and the other with the nature of moralism.

First, the political moralist offers rules to guide political decisions. But politics cannot be reduced to rules. It is an art that, like any other, calls for judgment to be practiced successfully. Such moralism fails as politics because it substitutes principles for prudence, which requires attention to the circumstances in which decisions are made. Political thinking must concern itself with how politics actually works, Geuss argues – not with how people should act based on some abstract ideal. And he thinks the same can be said of political theory, which, like the 'real politics' with which it is continuous, should be concrete, action-oriented, and partisan (Geuss, 2008, p. 95). Geuss, then, goes beyond Williams by denying the distinction between politics and philosophy. Political philosophy is politics under another name.

Second, Geuss argues that the political moralist imposes abstract standards on those who have no need for them. The word 'moralism', he writes, means 'a kind of moralised preaching and an associated assumption about the causal efficacy and cognitive significance of making moral judgements' (Geuss, 2015, p. 2). Moralists are busybodies whose intrusions into other people's affairs rest on shaky assumptions about the significance of their own pronouncements. The moralist, he argues, makes judgments of a specific kind: not judgments where the range of values that might be invoked is broad, varied, and undefined, but 'moral' judgments understood in Christian and Platonic terms as 'true' universally, eternally, and independently of 'their connection with the accidents of empirical existence and of history' (Geuss, 2015, p. 3). For Geuss, to be a moralist is to believe that there is a universal morality whose considerations override all others. But he is mistaken about this. Some moralists invoke a morality they regard as universal; others invoke the moral understandings of their own community. The moral critic has a multiplicity of places in which to stand.

The other element in traditional realism is 'reason of state', which holds that statecraft should be guided by state interests, not by moral ideals or fidelity to law. It is seen, by advocates and critics alike, as standing for the priority of expediency over morality in government and foreign affairs. But though reason of state may spring from moral scepticism, it does not presuppose it. Reason of state arguments are prescriptive, not meta-ethical. They are outcome-oriented or consequentialist: it is more important to achieve good results than to obey moral imperatives. Traditionally, reason of state was an argument about setting aside human (positive) law: no subject of God could set aside God's law, nor could any human being annul or alter natural law. An 'act of state', in international law, is one that is immune from the jurisdiction of any other state, but it can also be defined more broadly as a government act that is released from the usual legal constraints (Arendt, 2003a, pp. 37–39). This release does not arise, however, as a consequence of legal scepticism, which merely dismisses law as having anything other than a political meaning. To justify an official act as an act of state is to acknowledge the authority of the laws from which exemption is claimed, as when it is argued that a government can suspend ordinary laws in emergencies that threaten the legal order. Just as founding a state cannot be lawful under the laws of the state it replaces, maintaining a state can require extra-legal acts whose standard is not their legality but their efficacy. This is the central proposition of reason of state.

Most of those contributing to the new realism in political theory have given little attention to the 'classical realism' of twentieth-century writers on international relations who were concerned with reason of state or the long tradition of European legal and political thought on which they relied. These include Reinhold Niebuhr, Hans J. Morgenthau, John Herz, George Kennan, as well as others less famous, like Halford J. Mackinder, Nicholas Spykman and Georg Schwarzenberger, whose works are known today mainly to historians of international thought. Nor have those writing about the new realism in political theory given much attention to reason of state in constitutional matters – to questions of martial law, emergency powers and the relationship of sovereignty to law – about which there is a large and relevant literature (Dyzenhaus, 2006; Scheuerman, 2006).

To understand how the idea of reason of state works in these debates, it is helpful to distinguish between the moral and the prudential. For those who distinguish the two, to be related morally is to be related on the basis of rules. Moral rules are non-instrumental standards of right conduct. They prescribe obligations, regardless of whether those obligations advance or impede anyone's purposes. They are standards, moreover, whose authority is understood to be independent of the consequences of observing or not observing them: judging morally involves interpreting antecedently authoritative principles. To be related prudentially, in contrast, is to be related on the basis of interests. Prudential rules are maxims for advancing interests, instruments for producing desired outcomes whose authority depends on their utility for that purpose. And prudence involves calculating costs and benefits.

We can distinguish two versions of reason of state – one moral, the other prudential – according to how each justifies violating moral rules to achieve desired ends. What I'll call 'moral realism' reconciles morality with expediency in pursuing ends by arguing that policies designed to advance the welfare or security of the community are for that reason morally right. 'Prudential realism', in contrast, disdains to rationalise expediency in moral terms. It does not seek to 'justify' injustice – that is, show that it is 'just' – but argues instead that those who make decisions for the common good should do what is necessary, even in defiance of morality or justice. Better to admit honestly to having dirty hands, the argument goes, than to pretend one's hands are clean. For the prudential realist, morality and expediency are distinct, which means that the tension between them can be resolved only if one is given priority over the other.

In realist discourse, prudential arguments often appeal to 'necessity'. But that word cannot be taken at face value. If necessity means that an agent has no choice, the argument is fallacious because there are always alternatives in making a decision, no matter how unpalatable. If it means that the act chosen is indispensable to achieving a given end, attention is simply redirected the worth of the end and therefore to an ethical argument (Walzer, 2015, p. 8). Except in contexts in which it works as a term of art in deciding cases within the legal system, the appeal to necessity signals a move from a normal politics ruled by legal or moral constraints to an unconstrained politics of emergency, extremity, crisis or exception. Though it implies a sharp line between the normal and the exceptional, different realists seek release from those constraints at different points along a continuum from lawful to lawless conduct.

The new realism is seldom explicitly consequentialist, although a prudential concern with outcomes in the guise of a situational or 'all things considered' ethics is evident in frequent references to Max Weber's 'ethics of responsibility', which some take as justifying a politics of dirty hands. But those who casually invoke Weber on this point often fail to notice that his aim was not to defend an ethics of responsibility but rather to argue that to be a political leader was to be forced to choose between it and what he called an ethics of conviction: 'But whether we *should* act in accordance with an ethics of conviction or an ethics of responsibility, and when we choose one rather than the other, is not a matter on which we can lay down the law to anyone else' (Weber, 2004, pp. 91–92). Nevertheless, a realism based on the claims of politics might be expected to hold, and many political realists do hold, that public officials have distinctive responsibilities that make utilitarian or situation-specific reasoning appropriate in making decisions.

## What is the political in political realism?

Running through these discussions of reason of state is the suggestion that politics has a rationality of its own, which means that political activity is in some way different from other kinds of practical activity. We can ask, then, how political realists defend this proposition, and this will involve asking how they understand the word 'political'.

One answer is that political reasoning differs from practical reasoning only in that it is concerned with governing. Michael Oakeshott, for example, defines politics as the activity of making decisions in situations to which a government is expected to respond. It involves arguing about laws or policies by appealing to acknowledged principles or expected consequences. Conclusions about what a government should do depend on which principles are chosen and how they are interpreted and also on judgements regarding the desirability and likelihood of alternative outcomes. Because these considerations are complex and contested, political arguments are 'persuasive' rather than 'demonstrative' (Oakeshott, 1991, pp. 77–82). Arguments that invoke laws of history or other alleged necessities or unquestionable truths can be persuasive, he suggests, only when they are addressed to an audience that believes them. Totalitarian domination – or today, perhaps, social media – can create a discursive system in which shared beliefs are reinforced strongly enough to create an imagined world that is closed to alternative interpretations. But once that believing audience disappears, the 'closed real-imaginary world' in which such arguments make sense is likely to disintegrate (Oakeshott, 2008, p. 175).

Oakeshott sharply distinguishes theoretical from political discourse. He does not subscribe to the view that the new political realists share with the political moralists they criticise that the ultimate aim of theorising is practical guidance. But he would agree with the realist (he would say 'conservative') point that political activity requires judgement in interpreting rules and prudence in applying them. Such skills are acquired by experience and cannot be codified in such a way as to make experience unnecessary. Oakeshott also argues that decisions are not determined by facts any more than by rules, because facts are not given but are themselves products of interpretation. Appeals to moral absolutes, incontestable facts, alleged necessities, and the like are part of the rhetoric of persuasion, which in the end comes down to what you can get others to accept. Michael Walzer, defending the primacy of interpretation in moral and political discourse, makes a similar point when he argues that the 'discoveries' of Rawls and other philosophers are disguised interpretations of existing ideas and practices. 'No "proof"', he writes, 'takes precedence over the (temporary) majority of sages' (1987, p. 32).

Another answer to the question of how to define the political is that politics is a matter of conflict, power, and violence – a view espoused on both right and left by those who argue that liberal ideas obscure the true character of politics. In this they follow Carl Schmitt (2007), for whom politics is a zero-sum relationship of enmity that is incompatible with liberal ideas of legal order. What liberals call the rule of law is in fact the arbitrary will of a sovereign who, in deciding exceptions to law, also determines the law itself. It follows that the question of who is and who is not within the community of law is a matter of decision, not right. The argument on the left is that liberal ideas – parliamentary democracy, the rule of law, and liberal neutrality – are myths propagated by ruling elites to disguise their interests and therefore to dominate (Lilla, 2001, pp. 62–64). For them, liberalism is a form of false consciousness. Its real character is revealed only by the criticism of ideology, either from the standpoint of objective knowledge, as in 'scientific Marxism', or on the basis of a self-reflexive 'critical theory' (Geuss, 1981). Right and left converge, then, on the view that realist politics has little use for moral principles. Politics is disagreement, which for some means democratic politics and for others civil war (Honig, 1993; Mouffe, 2005). But if conflict is the essence of politics, everything is political – which is the main point on which right- and left-wing admirers of Schmitt agree. And if everything is political, the question of what distinguishes politics from other activities remains unanswered.

A third answer to the question of how to define the political is that politics is a way of dealing with conflict, one that emerges when the effort is made to distinguish political community from other kinds of community. According to one venerable view, a political community is a legal order, not a nation, an economy, or way of life. We distinguish political association from other kinds of community by calling it a state, which is historically and most intelligibly a legal concept, not a sociological one. Whatever their differences, those associated as citizens are subjects of the same laws that prescribe obligations and provide ways for dealing with failures to meet those obligations. But because a state is a non-voluntary association, it is morally important to distinguish between laws that respect individual freedom and those that suppress it in the name of some overriding interest or higher ideal. Political discourse must identify the boundaries between legitimate restraint and illegitimate oppression. Rawls and many others now condemned as anti-political moralists were concerned with this question, which is not one that realists can easily avoid. As the new realist debate unfolds, it is increasingly clear that 'order' means legal order and that legality implies legitimacy. Rawls and other liberals want to foreclose not politics, as the new realists accuse them of doing, but tyranny. It is hard to avoid the conclusion that treating people in a 'political' manner means respecting their claims not to be tyrannically used and abused.

The new realists have come to embrace Williams's view that politics must not only secure order but legitimise it (Williams, 2005, p. 3). This puts them at odds with the realism of Schmitt and others who define politics as conflict rather than as a way of dealing with conflict. What distinguishes Williams's view of the political from the liberal views he criticises is that it treats arguments for legitimacy as context-dependent and plural. Liberal conceptions of legitimacy, he argues, are not the only conceptions. Like Oakeshott, Williams observes that every justification is addressed to an audience and that different audiences expect different justifications. But despite this plurality, judgments of legitimacy must at some point identify 'the difference between political rule and mere domination' (Philp, 2012, p. 319). The question, as critics of Williams have observed, is whether this can be done without reverting to political moralism (Sleat, 2014, p. 315).

## The autonomy of the political

All these efforts to define the political assume that politics is autonomous, that it is independent of ethics. And those writing on the new realism seem to be converging on the view that it is this claim about the autonomy of politics that defines the realist perspective. But the claim is not unique to realism. Or, if it is, then the category of realism is much wider than one might suppose.

In his later writings, Rawls extends his understanding of legitimacy beyond liberal egalitarianism to articulate principles of legal order within a multicultural state as well as principles for the coexistence of liberal and non-liberal states. Surprisingly, he even embraces the realist argument that legal and moral constraints can be violated in emergencies. Agreeing with Walzer that Britain and the US were warranted in bombing German cities during the Second World War, Rawls argues that Nazi barbarism 'justifies invoking the supreme emergency exemption, on behalf not only of constitutional democracies, but of all well-ordered societies' (Rawls, 1999, p. 99). It is a mystery how Rawls could think that this argument could be part of a theory of justice, even a theory of 'political justice'. Hannah Arendt has it right when she condemns this sort of reasoning as opening a path towards evil. She rejects the consequentialist formula that one should choose the lesser evil, which is 'one of the mechanisms built into the machinery of terror and criminality … consciously used in conditioning government officials as well as the population at large to the acceptance of evil as such' (Arendt, 2003a, pp. 36–37). The 'supreme emergency exemption' is the sort of conventional formula that fits Arendt's definition, one that can open the door to evil for those unable to stop and think. Walzer acknowledges as much when he writes that 'emergency' and 'crisis' are 'cant words, used to prepare our minds for brutality' (Walzer, 2015, p. 251), and then relates how the British decision to destroy Germany's cities led step by step the firebombing of Japan and finally to dropping the atomic bomb on Hiroshima and Nagasaki. And, as Arendt observes, although the non-totalitarian world at first resisted the totalitarian idea of total war, with the obliteration of German and Japanese cities it came to embrace it, leaving an existential threat to future generations (Arendt, 2005, pp. 159–160).

Arendt's realism, if we can call it that, lies in her faith in the moral importance of 'thinking', by which she means the capacity to reason and understand, and which she contrasts with 'knowing', the claim to have verifiable knowledge. The distinction is crucial for comprehending and avoiding evil, Arendt thinks, because 'if the ability to tell right from wrong should have anything to do with the ability to think, then we must be able to "demand" its exercise in every sane person no matter how erudite or ignorant, how intelligent or stupid he may prove to be' (Arendt, 2003b, p. 164). This capacity to think must belong not only to the few who are professionally engaged in generating knowledge but to everyone. But, she argues, if thinking does not generate certainty, if it cannot accept its own results as axioms, then we cannot expect to find any unconditional (and therefore unquestionable) moral proposition, commandment, or code of conduct, 'least of all a new and now allegedly final definition of what is good and what is evil' (2003b, p. 167). Such absolutes cannot guide those who are lacking in judgment, and good judgment does not depend on their existence. Moral conduct is possible only when people 'start thinking and judging instead of applying categories and formulas which are deeply engrained in our mind, but whose basis of experience has long been forgotten and whose plausibility resides in their intellectual consistency rather than in their adequacy to actual events' (2003a, p. 37). In making judgement the foundation of political wisdom, Arendt was taking inspiration above all from Kant (Arendt, 1982).

Kant, along with Rawls, is a frequent target of new realist criticism. But like the later Rawls, Kant shares with the new realists a belief in the autonomy of the political, and in this sense his understanding of politics falls within the ambit of realism as defined by Williams and other realists for whom political principles are independent of moral ones. Williams criticises Kant (together with utilitarianism) for conceiving morality entirely in terms of obligation and implying that without morality there can be nothing but desire, force, and injustice. Morality, so understood, is a 'peculiar institution' detached from human experience – peculiar, presumably, because experience involves a multiplicity of ethical views and related considerations that are inescapably contextual and mutable (Williams, 1985, pp. 174–196). But for Williams the problem lies less with morality, which has a place as one perspective among others, than with philosophers who interpret its principles too literally or give them too much weight. To talk sensibly about politics, or about any other aspect of life, you have to know what's actually going on, and it is with this sense of the term 'real' that he defends political realism as the antidote to political moralism.

Kant would hardly disagree with most of this. His essay on theory and practice begins with a disquisition on the importance of judgement in practical reasoning (Kant, 1996a, p. 279), and he knew that he could not get a theory of politics from a theory of moral virtue. This is important because realist criticism of Kant is more often based on second-hand caricature than on careful attention to what Kant actually had to say about law and politics. We must therefore avoid being misled by the label 'Kantian'. As commonly used, that expression identifies a neo-Kantian applied ethics, a political ethics supposedly derived from the categorical imperative. But this is a misreading of Kant, who explicitly states that justice in relation to law and politics rests not on the categorical imperative (which is a principle of virtue, not justice) but on what he calls the 'principle of right' (Kant, 1996b, p. 387). The standard view of Kant, which many of the new realists share with the deontological liberals whose views they criticise, is at odds with readings of Kant that pay attention to the first part of the *Metaphysics of Morals*, which deals with what he called the theory of right, and it is to that theory that I refer. It may help to be reminded that Kantianism 'is an exceedingly amorphous term' in current philosophical writing and that 'virtually anyone may now qualify as a "Kantian" who subscribes to the values of freedom and equality as broadly conceived by Rawls' (Flikschuh & Ypi, 2014, p. 7). What, then, are the main elements of Kant's politics?

First, Kant's approach to politics is not applied ethics. In the *Metaphysics of Morals* and other late writings, he distinguishes right (or justice) from ethics (virtue), and he makes it clear that the theory of right is not an extension of his theory of ethics but rests on its own foundation. The principle of right is 'a postulate that is incapable of further proof' (Kant, 1996b, p. 388). Kant does not apply moral principles grounded on the categorical imperative to political life but grounds law and therefore political order on the requirements of the coexistence of embodied wills operating in space and time. Coexistence, however, implies at least the kind of justice that is inherent in the ideas of independence and non-domination.

Second, Kant views coercion as part of the definition of law and therefore as inherent in governing as the activity of enacting, interpreting, and enforcing laws. And governing is itself constrained by law. Coercion is not best understood as force (or the threat of force) added to a system of laws as a sanction for non-compliance, and therefore as secondary to legal obligation. It is inherent in the idea of law because legal obligations are non-voluntary. Acts that subject one person to the will of another are coercive, even if they do not involve force or the threat of force. And force is coercive even when (as in the case of self-defence) it is not a sanction or penalty (Ripstein, 2009, pp. 52–56). Coercion, then, is essential to law because law prescribes non-voluntary obligations. This suggests that although the word 'politics' can be used in various ways, at its core is the activity of deliberating the terms of a non-voluntary association – that is, its laws. The question of justice – of the 'rightness' of coercive law – is not the broad ethical question of how people should treat one another. It is the specifically political question of how they can justifiably be compelled to treat one another (Ripstein, 2004, p. 6). Just laws are rules that enable individuals to pursue their self-chosen ends without arbitrary interference by other individuals or by government. For Kant, just laws are laws that serve this 'civil' purpose and not, as in a corrupt or despotic state, particular private purposes.

Third, Kant's theory of politics is consistent with new realist efforts to ground liberal politics on an ethic internal to politics rather than on external moral principles arrived at by speculative reasoning. For Kant, that ethic rests on the idea of freedom as independence, which bars other people morally and should bar them legally from dictating one's purposes. Unlike other ideas of freedom, the idea of freedom as independence is not about agency in relation to the natural world or to one's own human powers. It is about agency in relation to other agents. What political theorists call negative and positive freedom, being agent-relative, can be notionally enjoyed in a state of nature but freedom as independence is social: it assumes the existence of other persons *against whom* one's freedom is asserted. For Kant, freedom as independence also assumes the existence of laws that prevent one person from interfering arbitrarily – that is, at will – with other people's choices, which would constitute domination. The legitimacy of a legal order depends on its having laws of this character.

Williams and other new realists leave more room than Kant does for different ways of legitimising political authority, but most would acknowledge that a legitimate regime cannot rest on *arbitrary* coercion: coercion that imposes the private interests of some on others, whether in private relations or by the state. Williams treats legitimacy as a matter of opinion but he thinks that people everywhere can recognise when power is being abused (Williams, 2005, p. 26). Legitimacy, he argues, can rest not only on beliefs of the sort that prevail in modern social democracies, but on a broader range of beliefs about the unacceptability of murder, torture, and other violations of human dignity (Williams, 2005, p. 69). Legitimacy, in other words, rests not on liberalism narrowly defined but on a view of legitimacy as entailing freedom from being dominated.

This idea of legitimacy is familiar to political theorists as the republican idea of liberty. And Kant's political thought is often characterised as republican. But there are differences. Kant's effort to ground republican liberty on the idea of justifiable coercion distinguishes his thought from recent efforts to revive republicanism. Republicans typically define independence empirically as the material power to avoid interference in pursuing one's ends. Kant, in contrast, defines independence as a relationship of moral right: it is the right not to be constrained by another's arbitrary choice (Kant, 1996b, p. 393). Independence is not a material condition but a moral one. It is violated if one's situation is one of arbitrary subordination to another's will, like that of the slave of a benign master, even if one is permitted to do what one likes. And one can be materially dependent on others in ways that do not violate one's right to independence. Similarly, domination is not the diminution of empirical freedom but a violation of rightful independence. It is wrong not because it harms an interest but because it violates a right.

Kant's politics is in this sense moralised, but as I have been arguing, this is also true of much of what is now considered political realism. The moralisation is framed in terms that are inherently political because they concern the conditions under which human beings can be said to be fellow subjects of a common law. A legitimate state is one that bars some from subordinating others for their own ends, which is close to Williams's definition of political order. This is not the full-blown liberal egalitarianism of the early Rawls but it is still a view of political order that excludes domination, as in the political liberalism of Rawls's later work. Kant's understanding of legitimacy, then, occupies a position somewhere between political moralism and political realism. But it avoids construing that position as a compromise between justice and reason of state, which would be an offence against justice. Acting unjustly for the good of the state cannot be brought within the scope of a theory of justice, even though unjust policies do not necessarily deprive a state of legitimacy. But if legitimacy is nothing more than belief in the acceptability of a political order, it is not the same as justice, for that acceptability may require no more than that the regime should conform to the mores of the community rather than to a more demanding moral standard. Justice requires more than a justification of that kind. We need to rescue the word 'justified' from its current use as a general term for a conclusion supported not by specifically moral reasons but by good reasons of any kind or by a balance of considerations. Because injustice cannot without self-contradiction be 'justified', that is, shown to be just, arguments for it must be based on something other than justice, simply as a matter of clarity and intellectual honesty. To say that an *unjust* act was 'justified' or 'justifiable' in the circumstances in which it was done is to speak loosely at best and at worst to deliberately blur the line that separates the just from the expedient.

A concern for truth and linguistic integrity, which for Williams is the point of realism, moves us away from a 'moral realism' that contradicts itself by asserting the justice of injustice towards a 'prudential realism' that is concerned with the conditions of legal order and therefore with creating and maintaining it. You cannot rule by law if there is no law. By addressing questions about the relationship between order, law, legitimacy, and justice, which are recurrent in the history of political thought, the new realism has an opportunity to mature beyond its attacks on moralism and liberalism to make a substantive contribution to political theory. But that contribution is unlikely to be novel because the tension between lawful government and policies designed to secure legal order is ancient and well understood. This leaves us about where we are now, beneficiaries of realism's rebuff of the simplistic moralising of academic political philosophy, together with a new appreciation of Rawls, and even of Kant, as more complex than they appear in realist discourse. At the very least, the new realism invites rethinking the expression 'political realism', which might help us to avoid the trap of using formulas and slogans as substitutes for thought.

## Acknowledgements

This paper was first presented at a symposium on Realism in Contemporary Political Theory sponsored by the Lee Kuan Yew School of Public Policy and the Department of Political Science, National University of Singapore. I want to thank Rahul Sagar for his leadership of the project and the Faculty of Arts and Social Sciences at NUS for supporting my work on it. I have learned from conversations with the symposium participants and subsequently with Christina Tarnopolsky and other colleagues in the Social Sciences Division at Yale-NUS, and from comments by an anonymous referee.

## Disclosure statement

No potential conflict of interest was reported by the author.

## References

Arendt, H. (1982). In R. Beiner (Ed.), *Lectures on Kant's political philosophy*. Chicago, IL: The University of Chicago Press.

Arendt, H. (2003a). Personal responsibility under dictatorship. In J. Kohn (Ed.), *Responsibility and judgment* (pp. 17–48). New York, NY: Schocken Books.

Arendt, H. (2003b). Thinking and moral considerations. In J. Kohn (Ed.), *Responsibility and judgment* (pp. 159–189). New York, NY: Schocken Books.

Arendt, H. (2005). Introduction into politics. In J. Kohn (Ed.), *The promise of politics* (pp. 93–200). New York, NY: Schocken Books.

Baderin, A. (2014). Two forms of realism in political theory. *European Journal of Political Theory, 13*, 132–153.

Dyzenhaus, D. (2006). *The Constitution of Law*. Cambridge: Cambridge University Press.

Flikschuh, K., & Ypi, L. (Eds.). (2014). *Kant and colonialism: Historical and critical approaches*. Oxford: Oxford University Press.

Galston, W. A. (2010). Realism in political theory. *European Journal of Political Theory, 9*, 385–411.

Geuss, R. (1981). *The idea of a critical theory: Habermas and the Frankfurt School*. Cambridge: Cambridge University Press.

Geuss, R. (2008). *Philosophy and real politics*. Princeton: Princeton University Press.

Geuss, R. (2015). Realism and the relativity of judgement. *International Relations, 29*, 3–22.

Herz, J. (1951). *Political realism and political idealism: A study in theories and realities*. Chicago, IL: The University of Chicago Press.

Honig, B. (1993). *Political theory and the displacement of politics*. Ithaca, NY: Cornell University Press.

Kant, I. (1996a). On the common saying: That may be correct in theory, but it is of no use in practice. In *Practical philosophy* (M. J. Gregor, Trans., pp. 277–309). Cambridge: Cambridge University Press.

Kant, I. (1996b). The metaphysics of morals. In *Practical philosophy* (M. J. Gregor, Trans., pp. 353–603). Cambridge: Cambridge University Press.

Lilla, M. (2001). *The reckless mind: Intellectuals in politics*. New York, NY: New York Review Books.

Mouffe, C. (2005). *On the political*. London: Routledge.

Oakeshott, M. (1991). *Rationalism in politics and other essays* (New and expanded ed.). Indianapolis, IN: Liberty Fund.

Oakeshott, M. (2008). Political laws and captive audiences. In L. O'Sullivan (Ed.), *The vocabulary of a modern European state* (pp. 168–180). Exeter: Imprint Academic.

Philp, M. (2012). Realism without illusions. *Political Theory, 40*, 629–649.

Pocock, J. G. A. (1975). *The Machiavellian moment: Florentine political thought and the Atlantic republican tradition*. Princeton: Princeton University Press.
Rawls, J. (1999). *The law of peoples*. Cambridge: Harvard University Press.
Ripstein, A. (2004). Authority and coercion. *Philosophy & Public Affairs, 32*, 2–35.
Ripstein, A. (2009). *Force and freedom*. Cambridge, MA: Harvard University Press.
Rossi, E. (2016). Can realism move beyond a methodenstreit? *Political Theory, 44*, 410–420.
Rossi, E., & Sleat, M. (2014). Realism in normative political theory. *Philosophy Compass, 9*, 689–701.
Scheuerman, W. E. (2006). Survey article: Emergency powers and the rule of law after 9/11*. *Journal of Political Philosophy, 14*, 61–84.
Schmitt, C. (2007). *The concept of the Political* (Expanded ed.). Chicago, IL: The University of Chicago Press.
Singer, P. (1972). Famine, affluence, and morality. *Philosophy & Public Affairs, 1*, 229–243.
Sleat, M. (2014). Legitimacy in realist thought: Between moralism and realpolitik. *Political Theory, 42*, 314–337.
Walzer, M. (1987). *Interpretation and social criticism*. Cambridge, MA: Harvard University Press.
Walzer, M. (2015). *Just and unjust wars: A moral argument with historical illustrations* (5th ed.). New York, NY: Basic Books.
Weber, M. (2004). Politics as a vocation. In *The vocation lectures* (R. Livingstone, Trans., pp. 32–94). Indianapolis, IN: Hackett Publishing Company.
Williams, B. (1983, November–December). The uses of philosophy: An interview. *The Center Magazine*, pp. 40–49.
Williams, B. (1985). *Ethics and the limits of philosophy*. Cambridge: Harvard University Press.
Williams, B. (2005). Realism and moralism in political theory. In G. Hawthorn (Ed.), *In the beginning was the deed: realism and moralism in political argument* (pp. 1–17). Princeton: Princeton University Press.

# Political realism meets civic republicanism

Philip Pettit

**ABSTRACT**
The paper offers five desiderata on a realist normative theory of politics: that it should avoid moralism, deontologism, transcendentalism, utopianism, and vanguardism. These desiderata argue for a theory that begins from values rooted in a people's experience; that avoids prescribing a collective deontological constraint; that makes the comparison of imperfect regimes possible; that takes feasibility and sustainability into account; and that makes room for the claims of democracy. The paper argues, in the course of exploring the desiderata, that a neo-republican philosophy of government does pretty well in satisfying them.

The aim of this paper is to construct a set of desiderata for a political philosophy – a normative theory for assessing political regimes – that deserves intuitively to be called realistic; and then to explore the case for thinking that civic republicanism is particularly well-suited to meeting those desiderata and of counting as a realist theory.

I equate civic republicanism with the Italian-Atlantic tradition that begins in the Roman Republic, is resuscitated in medieval and Renaissance Italy, fuels the English revolution of the seventeenth century and later the American war of independence. This tradition is marked by a belief, first, that the freedom of a person requires the absence of subjection to another's will, even the will of someone indulgent and well-disposed; and, second, that a polity that is required to support the freedom of all citizens – historically, a non-inclusive category – should be organized around a mixed constitution that gives citizens a contestatory as well as an electoral role. I am one of those who think that, suitably reworked, the tradition points us to a promising, neo-republican research program in politics. The main reworking needed derives from the requirement to take the citizenry to be inclusive: roughly, to include all adult, able-minded, more or less permanent residents.[1]

Political realism, as I understand it here, does not despair of normative theory and so is not a form of political skepticism or quietism or an error theory about political value. The core commitment is the claim that political philosophy should be shaped by the experience of people in the polity it addresses; should be tailored to the issues they face; should be cognizant of their potential for corruption and conflict; and should be able to guide them in their political aspirations and actions. In short, political philosophy should be essentially practical. That commitment supports a range of desiderata on a normative theory and I shall be looking at how far republicanism or neo-republicanism can satisfy them.

These accounts of civic republicanism and political realism are not uncontentious. Thus my characterization of political realism is silent on the question of whether the realm of the political is normatively autonomous, or indeed ontologically autonomous, despite the fact that this question is treated as central by some commentators (Rossi & Sleat, 2014).[2] And my account of the republican tradition is contentious in registering little or nothing about the contribution of Jean Jacques Rousseau.

Why treat political realism, in abstraction from autonomy issues, as a view about the practical form that normative theory should take? Because this construal reflects the main concerns of self-described political realists – this will become apparent later – as well as the intuitively related concerns of those who worry about confining political philosophy to the role of ideal theory.[3] And why restrict republicanism to the Italian-Atlantic tradition? Because this tradition focuses on the concerns of political realists, as we shall see, whereas the Rousseauvian does not. Rousseau retained the republican conception of freedom as non-subjection or non-domination but relied for advancing that ideal on the civic virtue of the citizens in a unified, sovereign assembly rather than on their ability to be able to contest and enforce a reconsideration of whatever is imposed on them, or proposed for imposition, by those in power (Pettit, 2013).

The paper is in five sections, corresponding to the five desiderata I identify. In each case I give an account of the desideratum and then look at how far neo-republicanism can meet it. I hope that the exercise will be of general interest, and not just of interest to those concerned with civic republicanism. It should help to elucidate some of the implications of political realism.

The desiderata that I associate with political realism fall into four categories since two of them, albeit worthy of concern in their own right, are logically connected: the satisfaction of 2b requires the satisfaction of 2a. Otherwise the desiderata are logically independent: it is possible for a theory to satisfy any one of them without satisfying the others.

(1) *Anti-moralism*. Political philosophy should begin from the concerns of people in the society for which it prescribes, not from an imported set of ethical principles.

(2a) *Anti-deontologism.* In extracting a normative ideal from those concerns, it should identify a collective target for the citizenry to track, not a collective constraint that they should satisfy.

(2b) *Anti-transcendentalism.* The ideal or set of ideals it adopts should be capable of guiding people's judgments of their actual society and their actions within it.

(3) *Anti-utopianism.* In putting forward those ideals for the guidance of members, it should focus on feasible initiatives and sustainable institutions, not just on ideal measures.

(4) *Anti-vanguardism.* And in putting forward those ideals, it should not pronounce on what is right and wrong without acknowledging the claims of democracy.[4]

## First desideratum: anti-moralism

Political realism is cast by its contemporary defenders as the antithesis of moralism. A moralistic approach would begin from the assumption that certain ethical or moral values are the relevant criteria for assessing possible, political arrangements – possible basic structures, in Rawls's (1971) terminology – regardless of whether or not those values are endorsed within the society. In Geuss's (2008, p. 8) words, it would make two assumptions: 'one can complete the work of ethics first, attaining an ideal theory of how we should act, and then in a second step, one can apply that ideal theory to the action of political agents'.[5] The approach would adopt an ethics-first policy, as he says, prescribing for the political world from a detached, presumptively universal standpoint.

Republicans are certainly opposed, as I see it, to this sort of moralism. They start from what I have described as the domination complaint, arguing that this complaint is ubiquitous in the world that most of us inhabit (Pettit, 2005). You will experience domination insofar as you find yourself subject to the will of another, however well-disposed towards you the other may be. In order to understand that complaint, it is necessary only to reflect on experiences that most of us will have had.

> Think of what it is to be in a position where you may or may not suffer ill-treatment, depending on the whim of another, be it a teacher or boss or bank manager, an insurance agent or a counter-clerk, a police officer or immigration official or prison warden. Think of what it is to have no physical or legal recourse against such an uncontrolled or arbitrary presence in your life; to be under the power of that other, depending on the goodwill of the person to avoid suffering some loss or harm. (Pettit, 2014a, p. xvi)

Think of your position in any such relationship, so the idea goes, and you will understand what it is to be dominated by another and, by contrast, what it is to escape such domination: to enjoy the freedom that goes with being your own master in the relevant sphere of choice.

The value of freedom as non-domination is not a philosopher's invention, then; it is an articulation of a concern that all of us have in our dealings with others. And it is a concern that naturally surfaces, not just in thinking about how we individually relate to other individuals or private organizations in social life, but also in thinking about how we relate individually and collectively to the government that rules over us, whether democratically or not; and about how we as a society relate to international entities: to other states, to international agencies, to multi-national corporations, and so on.

Or at least it is a concern that all of us are likely to have across these three fronts, social, democratic, and international, when we are not faced with famine or pestilence or total chaos. There is no denying that the concerns that drive us to politics are something of a luxury and that we cannot always expect people to enjoy the emotional and cognitive space to worry about how the local or international society is structured. Rawls (1971) describes the conditions required as the circumstances of justice, stipulating that in the society at issue people of limited altruism confront a society of only moderate scarcity.

But don't republicans suppose that freedom as non-domination is a universal and supreme value, thereby displaying a standard sort of moralism? Don't they hold that it retains its character and claims across an open-ended range of societies, past and present, and that it enjoys a pre-eminent place in relation to other values? They need not, and do not, view freedom in such a manner.

It is reasonable to hold that people are everywhere concerned with avoiding domination, as it is reasonable to hold that they are everywhere concerned with avoiding deprivation. This observation ought to be particularly congenial to political realists, since they inevitably emphasize the ubiquity of power imbalances and abuses. There is no society where involuntary subjection to the power of others can be welcome, as there is none where involuntary deprivation of material resources can be appealing.

The concern with avoiding deprivation may assume a different content in each social context, since it is a concern with having enough to make it possible to function in the local society, as Sen (1983) puts it: to have sufficient necessaries, in Smith's (1976, pp. 351–352) formula, to be able to live without shame before others and enjoy the status of a 'creditable person.' And similarly the republican concern with avoiding domination, in my construal of it, may assume a different content in each social context (Pettit, 2014b). In relations with your fellow citizens – in the domain of social justice – an un-dominated status is associated with being able to look them in the eye without reason for fear or deference (Pettit, 2014a, pp. 69–73). And the protection and resourcing that this requires is bound to be sensitive to differences in local culture, technology and expectations, and to impose quite different requirements across different periods and places (Pettit, 2014a, pp. 98–101).

But even if it is understood in this way, don't republicans have to take freedom as non-domination to be a supreme ethical good, thereby privileging an abstract ethical doctrine? Again, no. The tradition, as I read it, treats the value as a gateway good: a good such that, as a matter of empirics, if the institutions of a domestic society are designed to cope with problems of domination, then they will generally be designed to cope with a range of other problems too. Thus I argue elsewhere as follows.

> If we look after freedom as non-domination in the context of domestic legislation and government, guarding against people's dependency on others in areas of properly personal choice, then we will also have to look after goods like social, medical and judicial security, domestic and workplace respect and, more generally, a functioning legal and economic order. (Pettit, 2014a, p. xix)

Does republicanism do better in this first regard than other current philosophies of politics? On the face of it, yes. Take the concern with equality in the form it assumes when it is said that people ought to be enabled by their state to enjoy equality of resources (Dworkin, 2002), or equality of utility, or the sort of equality associated with Rawls's (1971) two principles. Rawlsian equality would impose roughly the following requirements: first, full equality for all in the protection of a basic set of liberties; and, second, the lowest level of socioeconomic inequality necessary to make the worst off better than the worst off would be in any more egalitarian society. However intellectually intriguing these values are, it is doubtful if they mirror concerns displayed in the same everyday and universal manner as the concern with not being under the power of others.

## Second desideratum: anti-deontologism

Every political philosophy with normative aspirations is bound to try to organize the ideas it marshals into a coherent, theoretical set of criteria for the assessment of political arrangements: that is what makes it into a philosophy as distinct from a political wish list. The second realist desideratum for a political philosophy is that in constructing values or principles to serve as criteria of assessment, it should not just provide us with a collective deontological constraint – a constraint that all citizens are required to satisfy together – rather than a collective teleological target.

Rawls's (1971, 1993) theory of justice offers the paradigm example of this approach. The issue he raises is how the members of a just society should be required to behave collectively: what principles they should be required by justice to satisfy as a body. This, equivalently, is the issue of what justice requires of the basic structure, assuming universal compliance. The answer he gives, of course, is that the members should be required to comply with his two principles of justice or, alternatively, that the basic structure should impose those principles on members of the society.

Why does Rawls take this approach? Primarily, because he thinks that what it is right for people to do or be required to do – how it is right that the basic structure should be be organized – has primacy over the question of the good that should serve as a criterion for assessing people's behavior or the basic structure under which they live. In more familiar terms, he looks in a purely deontological fashion for a constraint with which the just society should conform rather than looking in a consequentialist manner – or even in a consequence-sensitive manner (Sen, 2009) – for a target that it should promote.

The trouble with this purely deontological approach is that we are told nothing about what should happen if there is less than universal compliance: if, for example, the regime of Rawls's two principles of justice motivates a sizable number of wealthy people to do less than their best for the society. We may wish to condemn the wealthy for doing that (Cohen, 2008). But how should we respond if such condemnation is ineffective? What should we recommend when the constraint by which we define the ideally just society is likely to fall short of being implemented?

Rawls gives us no answer to this question, specifying the requirements of justice only for a society where people all conform to whatever is required of them. It is certainly of interest to know what any ideal would demand under one or another set of counterfactual conditions (Hamlin & Stemplowska, 2012). But it runs against the realist commitment to define the ideal only with reference to the perfect model, leaving it free of implications for how we should choose between societies that are likely in different degrees to satisfy it and, when they do so, to satisfy it in different measures.

This difficulty is not going to arise with any theory that identifies a single scalar value, or a more or less completely ordered set of values, that the citizenry are required to promote. Such a theory invites us to assess different political regimes, including those in which many do not contribute to the goal, on the basis of how far they are likely to realize that target, and to what extent. Such a value-target is likely to be enjoyed with a lower or higher degree of probability under different structures, and enjoyed there by fewer or more people, with greater or lesser intensity, over a smaller or larger extent. An approach based on such a target would let any polity be ranked according to its expected performance on that multi-dimensional metric, with suitable weightings being given to each dimension. Whatever criticisms it may attract as a theory of value, utilitarianism offers the classic example of this way of doing political philosophy.

As I interpret the tradition, republicanism is a target-centered, indeed consequentialist, approach of this kind. The equal enjoyment of freedom as non-domination is a scalar value by which we are invited to assess different regimes, including regimes that vary in the extent to which people in general, or people in special positions of power, are prepared to be compliant. There will certainly be difficulties involved in determining how relatively well those regimes are likely to do in avoiding domination, as there are difficulties involved in determining how relatively well societies are likely to do in reducing poverty. And in some cases it may even prove impossible to establish determinate rankings. But these difficulties reflect the multi-dimensional character of freedom as non-domination as well as the fact, as we have seen, that its interpretation in any society is sensitive to local standards. They are of little significance in comparison with the problems generated by a purely constraint-based philosophy of politics.

## Third desideratum: anti-transcendentalism

The fact that an ideal is defined within a model where people are unusually virtuous – say, committed to complying with whatever is required of them – does not strictly entail that it cannot serve as a guiding ideal for a world where people fall short of virtue (Valentini, 2009). It can serve in that role provided that it involves a target and not just a constraint, as we have already seen, and provided in addition that the target makes it possible to determine how far imperfect societies succeed in realizing it. Thus the defenders even of a targeted ideal need to show, first, that the ideal can be imperfectly simulated under non-idealized conditions; and, second, that it provides a metric for estimating how well these simulations do relative to one another and relative to the ideal. The third desideratum requires a political philosophy to be able to meet those conditions: not just to offer a target, as the second requires, but a target of a kind applicable in assessing regimes that approximate its realization only imperfectly.

This desideratum on political philosophy is particularly emphasized by Sen (2009), who castigates what he describes as transcendentalism. He argues that it is essential for any political philosophy to provide an ideal for ranking imperfect regimes, in particular the imperfect regime represented by the status quo. Unless a political philosophy can do this, it cannot serve to guide people in deciding about the political interventions they ought to pursue in their own society. This transcendental desideratum, as I understand it here, presupposes that the ideal hailed is targeted rather than constraining in character and imposes a more demanding condition than the anti-deontologism criterion.

Sen criticizes Rawls in particular for focusing on the perfect society – for taking a transcendental perspective – and for neglecting this requirement. Sen points out that having a transcendental ideal like Rawls's is not necessary for ranking imperfect arrangements against each other. Thus a Paretian criterion might enable us to say that one regime does better than another – it does better for some people and worse for none – without directing us towards any single ideal society. But the point he mainly emphasizes is that not only is a transcendental ideal like that embraced by Rawls unnecessary for comparing imperfect regimes; it is also insufficient. It does not enable us to rank actual regimes, since we are given no means of measuring how far actual, imperfect dispensations approximate the ideal.

But might we not rely on intuition to tell us how far different regimes fall from the Rawlsian ideal and how well they compare with one another? No, because of the general problem associated with the second best fallacy, as it is known. The fallacy is that of assuming that the closer an imperfect simulation is to a first-best ideal, in intuitive terms, the more likely it is to approximate that ideal (Goodin, 1995; Vermeule, 2011). Consider an ideal like that under which each citizen is treated as an equal, having access to equal influence within a system of control over government, and assume that a perfect democracy would satisfy this. And now think about two imperfect regimes. In one, everyone has access to the vote but campaign finance laws allow an elite to have a special oligarchical influence; in the other, control is vested in a group of people selected on a random basis every two years or so. The first regime simulates the perfect democracy much more closely in intuitive terms but it would be a mistake to think that it therefore approximates that ideal better than the second. On the contrary, the second looks much more likely to serve the guiding ideal – access to equal influence within a system of control – rather better than the first.

Simmons (2009) argues that, starting from Rawls's picture of a perfectly compliant world where justice is realized, we should develop principles for guiding the transition towards that world from the imperfectly compliant world we inhabit; we should identify principles for gauging which of the changes that we can bring about within the imperfect world would take us closer to the perfect. In maintaining this line, he identifies what would be needed for the approach to satisfy the anti-transcendentalism desideratum. But the problem is that the Rawlsian theory does not itself provide resources to enable us to generate the required principles.

Civic republicanism – strictly, civic neo-republicanism – does better. It argues that in order to enjoy equal freedom as non-domination people ought to be resourced and protected within a generous set of compossible choices, thereby enjoying social justice; that they ought to have an equal role in controlling the law that establishes those basic liberties, thereby enjoying democratic justice; and that as a society they ought to enjoy a generous set of compossible sovereign liberties that are established within a multi-lateral framework of international law: this would amount to their enjoying a republican version of international justice (Pettit, 2014a). It may not be possible in the abstract to say which of these dimensions is the most important but I assume that in any political predicament, it will usually be clear where the salient problems lie. There will certainly be trade-off difficulties in some cases, as an advance in one dimension threatens a retreat in another. But those are not inevitable and may even be relatively rare: it is not as if social, democratic, and global justice are in essential competition.

But does the neo-republican ideal offer effective guidance in each area on where to fix our sights in championing one or another intervention? I have argued elsewhere that the model of the republican *liber* or free-man, despite the masculinist connotations of the term, can guide us in elaborating workable heuristics to measure progress on social, democratic, and international fronts (Pettit, 2012, 2014a). Thus, as noted earlier, the system of social justice ought to enable each of us to look others in the eye without reason, by local standards, for fear or deference. The system of democratic justice ought to give each of us a reason for thinking that however far a public decision goes against us – however far it is unwelcome – that is just tough luck: it is not a sign of our living under an alien, potentially hostile will. And the system of international justice ought to give each society reason for straight talking in dealing with other states; it ought not to license the pretention of a master or require the servility of a dependent. That a regime fails one or another of these tests, and how far it fails the test, is likely to be perceptible to people within the society, notwithstanding the power of ideology. And when the failure is perceived, it ought also to be clear what changes, realistically achievable or not, would improve the situation.

## Fourth desideratum: anti-utopianism

The fourth desideratum associated with political realism is that not only should a political philosophy provide us with a targeted ideal that serves purposes of comparison between imperfect regimes; it should also direct us to regimes that are within feasible reach of our interventions and that establish sustainable institutions. It ought not to indulge in what we may describe as 'utopianism,' ignoring issues of feasibility and sustainability. There may be good intellectual reasons, of course, to look at what an ideal like Rawls's would require under infeasible or unsustainable conditions. The realist rejection of utopianism does not condemn the exploration of such an issue, only the assumption that that is the sole, or even the main business of political philosophy.

The idea behind the feasibility requirement is that people can only be normatively enjoined to adopt political interventions that they are able to implement, since 'ought' implies 'can.' This thought has to be central to political realism, since there would be no practical point in enjoining attempts to achieve the unachievable.

The lesson drawn from this idea is that political philosophers should give particular attention to reform proposals that are psychologically and institutionally within reach of the community to which they are addressed. There should be modes of individual and joint action identifiable, whether for those in government or those in the society at large, that would take the community towards the implementation of the proposals made. And those modes of action ought to be deliberatively accessible to the individual or collective agents involved: they ought to represent alternatives that those agents can regard as options – possibilities that are within their power to realize, depending on how their deliberation goes (Southwood, 2017).

There is bound to be great indeterminacy about the issue of what is feasible, and what not. It would be crazy to think that any proposal is infeasible if as a matter of psychology or sociology agents are unlikely to go along with it (Estlund, 2007). And equally it would be crazy to hold that any proposal is feasible so long as it is logically possible for people to implement it. Thus the floor constraint on feasible proposals should be higher than psychological or sociological likelihood and the ceiling constraint should be lower than logical possibility. But it is very hard to go beyond that and lay down an abstract criterion of feasibility. This is particularly so in virtue of the fact that normatively challenging a person or a group to do something may encourage and capacitate them, making what was previously infeasible into something that they now can do (McGeer & Pettit, 2015).

Our fourth desideratum not only requires a focus on feasible initiatives, it also prescribes a search for institutions that are capable, once established, of being reliably sustained. The idea here is that there would be little practical point – and nothing to attract political realists – in seeking to establish regimes that were unsustainable.

Whether an institution is sustainable in the relevant sense depends on the strains that it imposes on those who run the institution and those who are subject to it. But what exactly does sustainability require? That it be logically possible for people to sustain it, or that it be psychologically and sociologically likely that they will sustain it? In dealing with this question, it is possible to be a little less elusive than in dealing with the issue of feasibility. Assuming that the failure of an institution to prove sustainable is likely to have extremely negative effects – it may be a recipe for disenchantment and disorder – the sensible line is to set a high bar for whether an institution counts as sustainable. The line I suggest is that it should be able to survive across a range of inhospitable scenarios, many of them relatively improbable; in particular, it should be able to survive across scenarios where corruption sets in and those involved in the system depart from the most minimal standards of virtue.

Hume (1875, pp. 117–18) argued for this sort of line when he said that in 'fixing the several checks and controls of the constitution, every man ought to be supposed a knave, and to have no other end in all his actions than private interest.'[6] He may well have gone too far with this principle, since institutions that are fit to survive knaves may equally fail to inspire those who are more public-spirited: they may crowd out virtue (Pettit, 1997, Ch. 7). But the general point, surely supported by political realism, is that we should not design institutions that work reliably only so far as people generally prove to be relatively virtuous. We should economize on virtue, looking for arrangements that are more resilient in withstanding corruption (Brennan & Pettit, 2004); we should not rely on finding and empowering virtuous officials, for example, as in optimistic readings of what meritocratic selection can achieve (Bell, 2015). The arrangements we support should be capable of surviving the slings and arrows of our wayward nature and the obstacles it can put in the way of social progress.

Civic republicanism is wholly on side with the argument that political philosophy should give attention, if not exclusive attention, to feasible initiatives and sustainable institutions (Marti & Pettit, 2010). The tradition is marked, as we mentioned, by a commitment to the mixed constitution and a contestatory citizenry, where these are cast as requirements for avoiding the corruption of the state. The mixed constitution is defended on these grounds by Polybius, by Machiavelli, by Harrington, and of course by the authors of the *Federalist Papers*. In the traditional tropes, our human nature inevitably causes monarchy to degenerate into tyranny; aristocracy into oligarchy; and democracy into mob rule – ochlocracy, as Polybius calls it. Only the mixed constitution can guard against the corruption of individuals and institutions, according to the tradition. It provides the internal checks and balances, and the vigilance of a contestatory people, that can establish a powerful state without letting that power corrupt those in office.

The mixed constitution is not a blueprint for designing public institutions, of course, and taking it in that role has led to regimes with very salient problems, as with the problems of gridlock and oligarchy in the United States. But the idea signals a commitment within the republican tradition of thinking to guarding against a utopian disregard for the problems of feasibility and, in particular, sustainability. Here as on other counts I think that the approach has good realist credentials.

But do other contemporary philosophies fail to satisfy the requirements of the anti-utopianism desideratum? In practice, many do fail, since they routinely ignore issues of feasibility and sustainability in putting forward policies. And some make a principle of this practice. Cohen (2008) focuses on abstract questions of justice, for example – the pure theory of justice, so called – in conscious and assertive neglect of how justice is to be institutionally realized; he thinks that that issue is not one for philosophy proper. Rawls (1971) is a partial exception to this trend, for he devotes considerable attention to at least the sustainability question, asking whether a society that satisfied his two principles would be stable enough to continue in existence, attracting the support of its members.

## Fifth desideratum: anti-vanguardism

Vanguardists in the ordinary sense of the term seize power in the name of the people but exercise it without any concern for democratically registered views. Vanguardists in the sense I have in mind here do not seize power in the name of the people but they do pronounce on what it is right for the people to do. And, like their practical counterparts, they dictate what it is right for the people to do without regard for what is democratically supported. They speak to the members of the society, not in the tones of fellow citizens, but rather in the tones of the teacher or master: someone, quite simply, who knows more and knows better (Walzer, 1981). Vanguardism would license philosophers to make political recommendations that are not subject to the proviso that others should be willing to support the proposals democratically. There are some cases where the democratic proviso does not apply, as we shall see, but these are limited in range and number.

Let democracy be characterized at the most abstract level as a system that enables the citizens of a society – say, the adult, able-minded, more or less permanent residents – to share equally in exercising control over the laws and policies imposed on them by government. There are different sets of institutions that might claim to be able to deliver such equally shared control and the business of democratic theory is to explore and assess the rival candidates. Suppose that we endorse democracy within our political philosophy, arguing for the general value of equally shared control and defending one or another proposal for how to realize it. And suppose in particular that we argue that no regime can implement such control without giving equal electoral and contestatory rights to women and men. What should we say, then, about a society that operates under democratic procedures – perhaps even with the full consent of all involved – to deprive women of the vote?

In this sort of case we should condemn the step taken, regardless of the democratic support for the change. Democracy does not define democracy and even if men and women decide democratically on disenfranchising women, that does not make the resulting system democratic. Let democracy be taken as a value, then – a value, as republicans will think, that is rooted in people's concern for not being dominated – and it will put constraints on what a people may do: on how a *demos* may exercise its *kratos*. This argues, in my view, for constitutionally entrenching basic democratic rights, putting them beyond any possibility of being amended. Those rights would establish the claim of all citizens to be able to vote, stand for office, and contest political decisions by established channels, as well as the presupposed forms of claims to free speech and association. But I do not pursue this suggestion further in the present context.

This is to acknowledge that in the most basic aspects of democratic justice, philosophy can speak with a certain authority, basing its arguments on what is required for equally shared control of government. While those arguments will support certain policies in social justice – there can be no democratic justice without at least a basic education for all, for example, and a basic level of access to various material, social, medical, and judicial resources – this authority will not carry over to all the laws and policies that a government must consider. There are going to be any number of matters, whether in the spheres of democratic, social or global justice, on which a people may decide one way or another in such domains, consistently with citizens continuing to have equally shared control over those issues (Waldron, 2013).

If political realism involves the renunciation of an ethics-first philosophy, then it should inhibit theorists from claiming to speak on matters of these kinds with anything more than the authority of citizens among citizens. And this is a constraint that will impact deeply on common philosophical pretensions. Take even morally irresistible claims such as the claim that a government ought to provide for any area of the country that is subject to a natural catastrophe, or ought to ensure the welfare of the mentally disabled, or ought to contribute to alleviating famine abroad, or ought to put in place protections against the inhumane treatment of animals. We philosophers may feel very deeply about such questions, as indeed anyone is liable to feel deeply about them. But still, we ought to accept that in arguing for what our society and government ought to do, we have to recognize the legitimacy of democratic decision – if indeed there is a suitable degree of democracy in place – and contest standing practices only within the system. This may allow us to resort to civil disobedience but it will preclude any more radical rejection of the authority of ordinary people.

Opposition to philosophical vanguardism is part of the civic republican tradition, because the ideal of non-domination that republican theorists support has anti-vanguardist implications for the position they are entitled to assume in their theorizing. They may champion the equally shared control that a republican democracy would seek to institutionalize, brooking no opposition, however democratically supported. But they have to shrink from any pretention to impose their views on other people, however passionately they may hold those views. The guiding republican ideal requires them to assume the role of democratically respectful interlocutors who aim at persuading others, not overwhelming them.

This is in line with the longer tradition, in which the danger of public domination – the danger of domination by a government that is not suitably constrained by the people – bulks as large as the danger of private domination. The tradition has always emphasized, in the words of the eighteenth-century supporter of the American revolution, Price (1991, pp. 77–78), that 'however equitably and kindly' a popularly unconstrained government may treat its people, the domination it enjoys is inconsistent with freedom. This implies that philosophers have no right to expect that their prescriptions should be generally imposed by government, except to the extent that they are democratically endorsed by fellow members of the community (Pettit, 2015). They may speak with a certain authority on the basic requirements of democracy but they can speak only with the authority of citizens when they address other matters.

Does mainline political philosophy violate the desideratum of anti-vanguardism? Habermas (1995) and Forst (2002) satisfy the desideratum insofar as they distinguish between conditions, on the one side, that are required for realizing a structural ideal – equal democratic control or a universal right to justification – and conditions, on the other, that would be up for negotiation between people who lived under such an ideal. But many other philosophers clearly offend against the desideratum. They do so insofar as they follow the Rawlsian lead in looking at what justice requires of a society, without distinguishing between claims that are non-negotiable – that is, non-negotiably necessary for democratic control – and claims that are up for negotiation among the members of any suitably democratic society. Let justice be homogenized in this manner and vanguardism of the kind envisaged becomes inevitable (Pettit, 2015).

## Notes

1. The recent movement, as I think of it, began from the historical work of Skinner (1978) on the medieval foundations of modern political thought, and from his subsequent articles in the 1980's on figures like Machiavelli who wrote within the republican tradition identified by Pocock (1975). An up-to-date list of English works in neo-republican thought should include these books: (Brugger, 1999; Halldenius, 2001; Honohan, 2002; Lovett, 2010; MacGilvray, 2011; Marti & Pettit, 2010; Maynor, 2003; Pettit, 1997, 2012, 2014a; Skinner, 1998; Viroli, 2002); these collections of papers: (Besson & Marti, 2008; Honohan & Jennings, 2006; Kwak & Jenco, 2014; Laborde & Maynor, 2007; Niederbeger & Schink, 2012; Van Gelderen & Skinner, 2002; Weinstock & Nadeau, 2004); and a number of studies that deploy the conception of freedom as non-domination, broadly understood: (Bellamy, 2007; Bohman, 2007; Braithwaite, Charlesworth, & Soares, 2012; Braithwaite & Pettit, 1990; Laborde, 2008; Richardson, 2002; Slaughter, 2005; White & Leighton, 2008). For a recent review of work in the tradition see (Lovett & Pettit, 2009).
2. As it happens I have argued elsewhere for both sorts of autonomy, maintaining that the state is a corporate agent (List & Pettit, 2011; Pettit, 2012, Ch. 5) and that in seeking to promote republican freedom, it targets the achievement of a good that individuals could not bring about non-politically (Pettit, 2012, Ch. 3).
3. The two most prominent self-described realists are Williams (2005) and Geuss (2001, 2005, 2008, 2010). For a useful overview and critique of their work see (McKean, 2013). But on my characterization, realism also includes figures like Walzer (1981), in view of his opposition to philosophical hubris, and Sen (2009), in view of his critique of transcendentalism, as he calls it.
4. Desiderata 2, 3 and 4 correspond to three debates that Valentini (2012) takes to be involved, and often confused, in discussions of ideal versus non-ideal theory.
5. It is noteworthy that Cohen (2008) rejects the guidance assumption and represents a position that is diametrically opposed to political realism. For a useful discussion see (Valentini, 2009).
6. He may have been following Mandeville (1731, p. 332) who had earlier written that the best sort of constitution is the one which 'remains unshaken though most men should prove knaves.'

## Acknowledgments

Alison McQueen gave me very useful comments on an early draft of the paper, as did members of the Singapore workshop on a somewhat later version. The final paper benefited in addition from the suggestions of an anonymous referee and from those of Rahul Sagar. My thanks to all.

## Disclosure statement

No potential conflict of interest was reported by the author.

## References

Bell, D. A. (2015). *The China model*. Princeton, NJ: Princeton University Press.
Bellamy, R. (2007). *Political constitutionalism*. Cambridge: Cambridge University Press.
Besson, S., & Marti, J. L. (2008). *Law and republicanism*. Oxford: Oxford University Press.
Bohman, J. (2007). *Democracy across borders: From demos to demoi*. Cambridge: MIT Press.
Braithwaite, J., & Pettit, P. (1990). *Not just deserts: A republican theory of criminal justice*. Oxford: Oxford University Press.
Braithwaite, J., Charlesworth, H., & Soares, A. (2012). *Networked governance of freedom and Tyranny: Peace in East Timor*. Canberra: ANU Press.
Brennan, G., & Pettit, P. (2004). *The economy of esteem: An essay on civil and political society*. Oxford: Oxford University Press.
Brugger, B. (1999). *Republican theory in political thought*. New York, NY: Macmillan.
Cohen, G. A. (2008). *Rescuing justice and equality*. Cambridge, MA: Harvard University Press.
Dworkin, R. (2002). Sovereign virtue revisited. *Ethics, 113*, 116–143.
Estlund, D. (2007). *Democratic authority: A philosophical framework*. Princeton, NJ: Princeton University Press.
Forst, R. (2002). *Contexts of justice: Political philosophy beyond liberalism and communitarianism*. Berkeley: University of California Press.
Geuss, R. (2001). *History and illusion in politics*. Cambridge: Cambridge University Press.
Geuss, R. (2005). *Outside ethics*. Princeton, NJ: Princeton University Press.
Geuss, R. (2008). *Philosophy and real politics*. Princeton, NJ: Princeton University Press.
Geuss, R. (2010). *Politics and the imagination*. Princeton, NJ: Princeton University Press.
Goodin, R. E. (1995). Political ideals and political practice. *British Journal of Political Science, 44*, 635–646.
Habermas, J. (1995). *Between facts and norms: Contributions to a discourse theory of law and democracy*. Cambridge, MA: MIT Press.
Halldenius, L. (2001). *Liberty revisited*. Lund: Bokbox.
Hamlin, A., & Stemplowska, Z. (2012). Theory, ideal theory and the theory of ideals. *Political Studies Review, 10*, 48–62.
Honohan, I. (2002). *Civic republicanism*. London: Routledge.
Honohan, I., & Jennings, J. (Eds.). (2006). *Republicanism in theory and practice*. London: Routledge.
Hume, D. (1875). Of the independence of parliament. In T. H. Green & T. H. Grose (Eds.), *Hume's philosophical works*. London.
Kwak, J.-H., & Jenco, L. (2014). *Republicanism in Northeast Asia*. London: Routledge.
Laborde, C. (2008). *Critical republicanism*. Oxford: Oxford University Press.
Laborde, C., & Maynor, J. (Eds.). (2007). *Republicanism and political theory*. Oxford: Blackwell.
List, C., & Pettit, P. (2011). *Group agency*. Oxford: Oxford University Press.
Lovett, F. (2010). *A general theory of domination and justice*. Oxford: Oxford University Press.

Lovett, F., & Pettit, P. (2009). Neo-republicanism: A normative and institutional research program. *Annual Review of Political Science, 12*, 18–29.

MacGilvray, E. (2011). *The invention of market freedom*. Cambridge: Cambridge University Press.

Mandeville, B. (1731). *Free thoughts on religion, the church and national happiness*. London.

Marti, J. L., & Pettit, P. (2010). *A political philosophy in public life: Civic republicanism in Zapatero's Spain*. Princeton, NJ: Princeton University Press.

Maynor, J. (2003). *Republicanism in the Modern World*. Cambridge: Polity Press.

McGeer, V., & Pettit, P. (2015). The hard problem of responsibility. In D. Shoemaker (Ed.), *Oxford studies in agency and responsibility* (Vol. 3, pp. 160–188). Oxford: Oxford University Press.

McKean, B. (2013). *What makes a fiction inconvenient? On the political realisms of Raymond Geuss and Bernard Williams. Political Theory Workshop*. Chicago, IL: University of Chicago.

Niederberger, A., & Schink, P. (Eds.). (2012). *Republican democracy: Liberty, law and politics*. Edinburgh: Edinburgh University Press.

Pettit, P. (1997). *Republicanism: A theory of freedom and government*. Oxford: Oxford University Press.

Pettit, P. (2005). The domination complaint. *Nomos, 86*, 87–117.

Pettit, P. (2012). *On the people's terms*. Cambridge: Cambridge University Press.

Pettit, P. (2013). Two republican traditions. In A. Niederberger & P. Schink (Eds.), *Republican democracy: Liberty, law and politics* (pp. 169–204). Edinburgh: Edinburgh University Press.

Pettit, P. (2014a). *Just freedom: A Moral compass for a complex world*. New York, NY: W.W. Norton.

Pettit, P. (2014b). Republicanism across cultures. In J.-H. Kwak & L. Jenco (Eds.), *Republicanism in Northeast Asia* (pp. 15–38). London: Routledge.

Pettit, P. (2015). Justice, social and political. In D. Sobel, P. Vallentyne, & S. Wall (Eds.), *Oxford studies in political philosophy* (Vol. 1, pp. 9–35).

Pocock, J. G. A. (1975). *The machiavellian moment: Florentine political theory and the atlantic republican tradition*. Princeton, NJ: Princeton University Press.

Price, R. (1991). *Political writings*. Cambridge: Cambridge University Press.

Rawls, J. (1971). *A theory of justice*. Oxford: Oxford University Press.

Rawls, J. (1993). *Political liberalism*. New York, NY: Columbia University Press.

Richardson, H. (2002). *Democratic autonomy*. New York, NY: Oxford University Press.

Rossi, E., & Sleat, M. (2014). Realism in normative political theory. *Philosophy Compass, 9*, 689–701.

Sen, A. (1983). Poor, relatively speaking. *Oxford Economic Papers, 35*, 153–168.

Sen, A. (2009). *The idea of justice*. Cambridge, MA: Harvard University Press.

Simmons, A. J. (2009). Ideal and non-ideal theory. *Philosophy and Public Affairs, 38*, 5–36.

Skinner, Q. (1978). *The foundations of modern political thought*. Cambridge: Cambridge University Press.

Skinner, Q. (1998). *Liberty before liberalism*. Cambridge: Cambridge University Press.

Slaughter, S. (2005). *Liberty beyond neo-liberalism*. London: Macmillan Palgrave.

Smith, A. (1976). *An inquiry into the nature and causes of the wealth of nations*. Oxford: Oxford University Press.

Southwood, N. (2017). Does 'ought' imply 'feasible'? *Philosophy and Public Affairs, 45*.

Valentini, L. (2009). On the apparent paradox of ideal theory. *Journal of Political Philosophy, 17*, 332–355.

Valentini, L. (2012). Ideal vs. non-ideal theory: A conceptual map. *Philosophy Compass, 7*, 654–664.

Van Gelderen, M., & Skinner, Q. (2002). *Republicanism: A shared European heritage*, 2 vols. Cambridge: Cambridge University Press.

Vermeule, A. (2011). *The system of the constitution*. New York, NY: Oxford University Press.

Viroli, M. (2002). *Republicanism*. New York, NY: Hill and Wang.

Waldron, J. (2013). Political political theory: An inaugural lecture. *Journal of Political Philosophy, 21*, 1–23.

Walzer, M. (1981). Philosophy and democracy. *Political Theory, 9*, 379–399.

Weinstock, D., & Nadeau, C. (Eds.). (2004). *Republicanism: History, theory and practice*. London: Frank Cass.

White, S., & Leighton, D. (Eds.). (2008). *Building a citizen society: The emerging politics of republican democracy*. London: Lawrence and Wishart.

Williams, B. (2005). *In the beginning was the deed: Realism and moralism in political argument*. Princeton, NJ: Princeton University Press.

ə OPEN ACCESS

# Political realism as ideology critique

Janosch Prinz and Enzo Rossi

**ABSTRACT**
This paper outlines an account of political realism as a form of ideology critique. We defend the normative edge of this critical-theoretic project against the common charge that there is a problematic trade-off between a theory's groundedness in facts about the political status quo and its ability to envisage radical departures from the status quo. To overcome that problem, we combine insights from theories of legitimacy by Bernard Williams and other realists, Critical Theory, and analytic epistemological and metaphysical theories of cognitive bias, ideology and social construction. The upshot is an account of realism as empirically informed critique of social and political phenomena. We reject a sharp divide between descriptive and normative theory, and so provide an alternative to the anti-empiricism of some approaches to Critical Theory as well as to the complacency towards existing power structures found within liberal realism, let alone mainstream normative political philosophy, liberal or otherwise.

## Introduction

The accusation of status quo bias is a major obstacle in realism's path. Even theorists who are friendly to the realist enterprise express worries as to the approach's ability to radically *criticise* the reality to which, in some important sense, any realism worth its name must be tied. When it comes to *prescribing* alternative political scenarios this problem becomes, predictably, even more pressing. Crudely, there appears to be a problematic trade-off between a theory's groundedness in facts about the status quo and its ability to consistently envisage radical departures from the status quo. Or so the criticism goes.

In this paper, we respond to that criticism by outlining an account of realism as ideology critique. More specifically, we investigate one avenue of realist defence against the status quo bias accusation: the idea that, if an empirically informed analysis of the status quo is guided by an appropriate theory of ideology, it can yield a normative indictment of the status quo and, in some cases, even an account of a desirable alternative state of affairs. Here, the challenge is to make criticism of ideology compatible with the realist rejection of moral principles external to the context and problem in question. And so we see an affinity between the realist project and the long-standing tradition of 'immanent critique' in Critical Theory. Moralist critique of institutions or practices can be internal in the sense it is still committed to articulating the normative commitments that *ostensibly* underpin those institutions and practices (think of the enormous liberal literature on what kinds of first-order political principles most truly express liberalism's normative commitments). Realist or immanent critique, on the other hand, seeks to transcend, transform, or even subvert those commitments without thereby relying on further, external moral standards. Put differently, immanent critique is *internal to the political context without being internal to the ideology that underpins that context*. In our specific account of realist ideology critique, this critical standpoint will be reached by relying on epistemic rather than moral commitments.

To make space for such an understanding of critique, we will reject some of the dichotomies that have pervaded recent debates about the self-conception of political theory, especially those between normative and descriptive theory, and between realism and radicalism. To wit, this involves rethinking the relationship of political theory to its political and social context in terms of the sources of normativity, the role of self-reflection, and the purposes of theorising.

On our understanding, realism aims both at action-orienting normative evaluation *and* at diagnostic critique. That is why we question the division between normative and descriptive forms of political theorising. In order to achieve this dual aim of diagnosis and evaluation, realist political theory needs to incorporate a wider understanding of what constitutes a normative approach besides making prescriptions. Ideology critique bases its normative evaluations on the diagnosis of specific problems, and so offers one way to challenge the aspiration of critical distance via an 'uncluttered view' (Rawls, 2005, p. 20), which has been very influential in post-Rawlsian political theory. An 'uncluttered view' embodies the problems of excessive abstraction and idealisation (Mills, 2005). What is more, criticism of ideology is committed to self-reflection with regard to how normative and epistemic concerns are intertwined, thus it addresses the political import of political theory itself. So we contend that the combination of realism and criticism of ideology opens up the space for rethinking the potential of realism as a distinctive approach to political theory.

We begin the first section with a brief, working characterisation of realism, and we set out the status quo bias charge. We then discuss the most developed response to this charge in current realist literature, namely Bernard Williams' 'Critical Theory Principle'. We argue that, while the Critical Theory Principle is a pioneering step in the right direction, it does not contain a sufficiently developed account of ideology to succeed. In the second section, then, we spell out the desiderata for a successful realist account of ideology. On that basis, we outline such an account by combining elements from recent Frankfurt School-inspired Critical Theory and from contemporary analytic epistemological and metaphysical discussions of ideology and social construction. The upshot is an understanding of criticism of ideology, which delivers tools for meeting realist commitments to diagnosing the patterns of power exercise, while thus preparing the basis for a non-moral criticism of the social and political order. In the third section, we summarise our argument and canvass a few questions for further work on realism as ideology critique.

## Realism and the status quo

Let us start by distinguishing between two incompatible *Idealtypen* of realism found in the growing literature on the topic. On one view, realism is merely a subset of nonideal theory. The idea is that realists 'are looking for principles which are likely to be effective here and now' (Valentini, 2012, p. 660). So realism can be a distinctive view only insofar as it picks out a specific subset of feasibility constraints (e.g. those to do with power) that are sometimes overlooked by mainstream, Rawlsian nonideal theory (Baderin, 2014). Or perhaps realism can bypass reference to an ideal when devising the nonideal, along the lines of Sen's 'comparative' approach to justice (Raekstad, 2015). On another, more classical view,[1] realism breaks with contemporary anglophone political theory's moralistic tendency to proceed as a branch of applied ethics (Geuss, 2008, Williams, 2005). Here, the general idea is that the sources of political normativity are not – or not exclusively – to be found in pre-political moral commitments, but in a form of normativity inherent to politics (Jubb & Rossi, 2015; Rossi & Sleat, 2014; Sleat, 2014). Hybrid views exist as well (Galston, 2010; Hall, 2016; Jubb, 2015).

Adjudicating the relative merits of each of those approaches is beyond the scope of this paper. At any rate, given the question at hand – whether realism has a built-in status quo bias – it will be natural to take as our reference point the more classical conception of realism, the one that sets it apart from nonideal theory. There are two reasons for this choice. First, whatever the attractions of nonideal theory, it is explicitly anchored in the status quo, insofar as it is primarily concerned with balancing normative aspirations against feasibility constraints. That is not to say that a series of feasible incremental changes ('transitional' nonideal theory) can never lead to profound social and political transformations. The point is just that nonideal theory largely wears its relationship to the status quo on its sleeve, so there can be no general answer to the question as to whether a whole family of nonideal theories has a bias-inducing relationship to the status quo. Each nonideal theory will (or at least should) furnish its own answer, through its account of exactly how to accommodate feasibility constraints. Second, and more importantly, the classical view of realism presents a potentially more rewarding challenge. It is not particularly surprising that one can call for a radical transformation of politics by invoking moral commitments that sit outside of politics (even when those commitments have to be implemented via a series of feasibility-conscious steps). Indeed, realists argue that moralist radicalism is just too easy, or a category mistake (Rossi 2010, 2015, 2016).[2] Such moralist radicalism is typically not interested in connecting to the specific motivations and patterns of action as they are mediated through the understanding of politics in a particular context. This lack of connection can lead to pernicious actions in the name of the prescriptions of moralist radicals that distort their intentions (if not their principles), or, if moral radicalism altogether fails to connect to its addressees, lead to little practical importance. The more probing challenge for a concretely action-guiding political theory is to start the generation of its normative purchase from within the understanding(s) of politics to be found in the context(s) of action in question. This involves examining the presuppositions of any normative claims, including those that seek to claim that their validity is pre-political, i.e. not tied to the specificities of the context. This is why we seek to show that realists can call for radical change while drawing on resources immanent in, rather than external to, the political practice they criticise.

But why, exactly, is classical realism routinely accused of status quo bias? Here is one (somewhat sympathetic) critic's take on the problem:

> ... if, as realists, we place emphasis on historically constant factors which we regard as constraints on political possibility – and if our main objection to the liberal mainstream is that it overlooks these factors – then our realism will inevitably tend to nudge us towards a greater acceptance of the status quo ... Of course, it is *logically* quite possible to emphasise 'stability' (rather than 'justice' or 'equality') as a political aspiration, and at the same time to call for far-reaching social change, or even revolution, as the means to that end. But if – as I would suggest is the case – realists generally do no such thing, but rather preserve the areas where mainstream liberal theory affirms the status quo (e.g. its acceptance of the basic framework of liberal democracy) whilst eliminating the points where liberal demands most visibly exceed what is actually realised within that framework (e.g. by prescribing a significantly greater degree of material and social equality), then realism is a de facto conservative force in political theory. (Finlayson, 2015, pp. 7–8)[3]

Note that this is not simply a denunciation of excessive attention paid to feasibility constraints. Though that passage arguably collapses the distinction between nonideal-theoretic and classical realism, it latches on to some important features of the latter: classical realists do place emphasis on constants in the realm of politics, most notably on features often wished away by moralist theory such as coercive power relations (Sleat, 2014). Within realism, though, coercion is best understood not primarily as a feasibility constraint, but rather as a constitutive feature of any political practice. Feasibility constraints are not unwelcome hindrances. For realists, coercion is not an obstacle to be removed or bypassed. The question of achieving political results without coercion (e.g. through consent) is ill posed. The art of politics just is, to a large extent, the art of coercing with good judgement – of distinguishing between good and bad coercion. So the problem here is whether this realist understanding of politics is tantamount to status quo bias. More generally, the problem is whether realists' commitment to working within the parameters of a sphere of politics with its own normative standards limits their political imagination.

First, as long as realists engage their moralist (liberal or not) opponents in discussions about the *nature of the political* and especially if their characterisations are based on assertions, e.g. of the conflictuality of politics, the limitation of the political imagination is a plausible impression. Such attempts at getting an accurate picture of the political (McNay, 2014) and then issuing prescriptions that meet this characterisation are questionable, and do not warrant claims to a greater degree of prescriptive and descriptive fit, nor a claim to settling ontological questions of what is real (Little, 2015). If anything, this issue marks a starting position for understanding how politics is a thick evaluative concept (Jubb & Rossi, 2015) – and even for this goal realists could consult sources that actually study how political speech and action can be distinguished from non-political speech and action (Freeden, 2013).

Second, the source of normativity does not necessarily prefigure the stance of a political theory to its political context. Moralism can be connected to radical political goals (think of utopian animal rights ethicists) or may be status quo supporting, as Geuss (2005) argues for Rawlsianism. Likewise, realism may support a broad range of positions towards the status quo.[4]

While some general, in-principle defences of the emancipatory or radical potential of realism have been put forward (e.g. Geuss, 2010a; Prinz, 2015a, Rossi 2010, 2015), Bernard Williams' theory of legitimacy[5] remains the main systematic attempt to explain how one may tackle a classic problem of normative political theory within a realist framework. So for our purposes, Williams' theory of legitimacy is an explorative exercise into how one may criticise a set of political practices or institutions while remaining committed to evaluating them with standards internal to political practices themselves.

Williams' first move is to delimitate the sphere of politics by identifying a 'first political question', namely 'the securing of order, protection, safety, trust, and the conditions of cooperation.' (2005, p. 3). But, unlike in Hobbes, solving the first political question is a necessary but not sufficient condition for a polity's legitimacy. To achieve legitimacy, a polity must meet what Williams calls the 'Basic Legitimation Demand' (BLD): 'Meeting the BLD can be equated with there being an "acceptable" solution to the first political question.' (2005, p. 4). In order for a solution to the political question to be "acceptable", those subject to it have to be able to make sense of it as such a solution.

For Williams, 'making sense' is 'a category of historical understanding, [...] a hermeneutical category' (2005, p. 11) which assesses whether the legitimation being used can be understood within the context (including its concepts) to which it is addressed. More precisely, however, the idea is about checking whether an 'intelligible order of authority makes sense to us as such a structure' (2005, p. 10) which 'requires [...], that there is a legitimation offered which goes beyond the assertion of power'. Williams adds that 'we can recognise such a thing because in the light of the historical and cultural circumstances [...] it [makes sense] to us as a legitimation' (2005, p. 11). This qualification underscores Williams' commitment to contextualism. However, it also invites worries about the standing of the idea of 'making sense' to evaluate rationales of legitimation.

This idea relies on 'our' ability to differentiate legitimations based on assertions of power from legitimations for the endorsement of which there are reasons other than their hold of power over us. To flesh out this distinction and render it politically viable, Williams introduces his 'Critical Theory Principle' (CTP): 'the acceptance of a justification does not count if the acceptance has been produced by the coercive power which is supposedly being justified' (2002, pp. 219–232, 2005, p. 6). For Williams, 'the difficulty with [this principle], of making good on claims of false consciousness and the like, lies in deciding what counts as having been "produced by" coercive power in the relevant sense' (2005, p. 6). This commits Williams to looking at the actual beliefs of people, who accept the legitimacy of a regime only because they have not come to realise yet that there are no other reasons to accept it as legitimate than the power of this regime over them to accept it as legitimate (Williams, 2002, p. 231), not simply as they are now, but from the point of view of their transformation (and not simply as they are now):

> If we are supposing that the background is simply these people's current set of beliefs, then almost anything will pass the [Critical Theory Principle] test (except perhaps some cases of extreme internal incoherence). If we suppose, on the other hand, an entirely external frame of reference, then nothing very distinctive is achieved by the test. We need a schema by which we start with the people's current beliefs and imagine their going through a process of criticism, a process in which the test plays a significant part. (2002, p. 227)

The schema which Williams endorses and which helps with clarifying what 'counts as having been "produced by" coercive power in the relevant sense' (2005, p. 6) is based on an idea which has been called 'reflective unacceptability' (Geuss, 1981, pp. 55–65). This entails encouraging a process of reflection in people on whether they would still hold on to their beliefs (directly or indirectly about the legitimacy of the regime), once they had realised how they came to hold them. This process will lead to context-sensitive evaluations based on reasons actually available to the relevant agents. However, while the Critical Theory Principle enables Williams to offer some protection against internalised oppression 'making sense' and passing as legitimate, this arguably comes at the price of a tension with Williams' realist commitments. Williams' contextualism could be taken to imply that he seeks to develop criteria for legitimacy without recourse to a framework of justification based on moral criteria unmediated by the particular political context. This does not imply that Williams rejects moral criteria per se, but rather that he rejects criteria for legitimacy that are 'doubly moral', i.e. moral in substantive content and moral in terms of the reasons why they are brought forward. Williams rejects the latter sense of 'moral' for at least two reasons: Firstly, he views the demand for legitimation as initiated primarily by political, not moral considerations (Williams, 2005, pp. 3–6). Secondly, given the conditions of pluralism which obtain in modern societies, it would be difficult to individuate moral criteria that can hover above the political fray without undermining said pluralism (see Schaub, 2012, pp. 445–447). If this distinction is applied to his discussion of the Critical Theory Principle, the question is if the moral criteria that are introduced are sufficiently mediated through the political context. Concretely, moral criteria enter the Critical Theory Principle test in through Williams' morally charged assessment of the situation in which the state fails the test as one of 'injustice' (Williams, 2002, p. 231). This assessment arguably relies on an idea about the moral standing of agents, which is unjustly violated through the abuse of power. This could be linked to the understanding of 'power as right', which holds that authority only springs from power if power is exercised in accordance to moral and legal right (Hindess, 1996), irrespective of the specificities of the context.

This assessment of 'injustice' could also be viewed to connect to the moral ideal of autonomy, which Williams might have more or less accidentally brought in from Critical Theory when constructing the Critical Theory Principle. This is particularly visible in Williams' hope that the Critical Theory Principle help the disadvantaged realise the 'most basic sense of freedom, that of not being in the power of another' (2002, p. 231). This seems to imply a near total lack of freedom in a situation in which the polity fails the Critical Theory Principle test – perhaps a way to displace the question of whether the mere fact of a coercively generated belief automatically disqualifies it from providing legitimacy. But the move may seem rather quick. It may be a problematic assumption about the totality of power typical of key texts of Critical Theory and the early Foucault (see Honneth, 1993). Williams' hope, even on a minimalist construal, could then be seen as receiving some of its appeal from the moral ideal of autonomy, especially in cases where 'being in the power of another' is not a matter of physical captivity but rather a limitation of the (mental, social etc.) development of the persons in question – a matter of ideology's ability to induce 'voluntary servitude' (Rosen, 1996).

Arguably, this interpretation is in tension with Williams' understanding of the political (rather than moral) value of liberty (2005, chapters 6 and 7). Within Williams' realism, the injustice might be viewed to refer to the fact that the abuse of power makes it – in the long run – impossible for those suffering from it to enjoy the benefits of politics in the full sense of the term. Those benefits at least entail that the first question of politics – the 'securing of order, protection, safety, trust, and the conditions of cooperation' (2005, p. 3) – is answered. More precisely, the way out of the problem would be to stress the work done by the very *concept* of politics. Raw domination of the sort endured by the Helots in Sparta just isn't politics, and this is a conceptual rather than a moral claim. (Hall, 2015; Sagar, 2014; Williams, 2005, p. 5).

Still, the worry remains that the Critical Theory Principle – introduced by Williams to prevent his 'make sense' criterion of legitimacy from sanctioning political orders whose acceptance is based on (the abuse of) their existing power – succeeds at the price of relying on a moralised definition of politics.

To put it another way, it is questionable whether we can anchor a whole theory of ideology to a conceptual claim about the nature of politics, given that the concept of politics is itself essentially contestable, and decontestation is achieved precisely through ideologies' ability to highlight or even introduce a concept's normatively controversial connotations (Freeden, 2013). We have no usable concept of politics (or freedom, or equality) until we decontest it, i.e. we flesh out its meaning by reference to a wider set of normative commitments. If, say, 'freedom' means one thing to liberals and another to socialists, then 'politics' may just mean one thing to realists and another to moralists. The moralist may well maintain that politics can include raw domination, and that would be precisely why we need moral standards to guard against the excesses of politics. And so the question re-emerges as to whether the contentious normative connotations used by Williams in his decontestation of the concept of politics do not themselves originate in pre-political moral commitments.[6] It looks as though Williams oscillates between admitting only those moral criteria mediated through the valuations of a political context and buying the critical-normative edge of his view of legitimacy at the cost of a lapse back into moralism, i.e. by admitting moral criteria and conceptual stipulations that are unmediated by a particular political context. We maintain that in order to generate a distinctively realist form of critical purchase which is compatible with the goal of contextual action-guidance, a stronger case for the compatibility of contextualist and critical commitments is required.

## Radical realist ideology critique

If Williams' attempt to dispel the worry of status quo bias while remaining true to realism fails, it fails in an illuminating way.[7] So, before discussing options to fill in the gaps in Williams' Critical Theory Principle, let us set out the desiderata for a successful realist account of ideology critique.

The appeal of Williams' Critical Theory Principle lies in the general thought that there is something wrong with trying to justify a sociopolitical system through a normative commitment that is itself a direct product of the coercive power relations within that system. As Williams puts it,

> if one comes to know that the sole reason one accepts some moral claim is that somebody's power has brought it about that one accepts it, when, further, it is in their interest that one should accept it, one will have no reason to go on accepting it. (2002, p. 231)

Formulating the point in terms of the specific interests of some groups may be overly controversial, insofar as it introduces further normatively charged elements into the picture, and might even have a not exactly ecumenical Marxian ring to it. Besides, one may worry about the familiar genetic fallacy: might the truth not happen to be aligned with the interests of the powerful, at least sometimes? But the general appeal of the point can be preserved by presenting it as more of a matter of epistemic bias: crudely, we do not let rulers set the standards of legitimacy for the same reasons that we do not let authors referee their own papers. We do not need to spell out exactly why the perspective of the authors or rulers is flawed, but only why it carries an epistemic risk. In other words, we need to work out what are the properties of beliefs[8] such that, once they have been uncovered, undermine credence in the belief at hand.

The account of ideology we require to underpin our theory of realism as ideology critique, then, has three main desiderata: (i) it must avoid moralised versions of salient political concepts (realistic desideratum), (ii) it must steer clear of the genetic fallacy (critical desideratum) and (iii) it must offer a broad framework for generating evaluative criteria for the social order in question (evaluative desideratum).

The realist desideratum's purpose is to allow the critic to distance herself methodologically from the object of critique. One may see this as a familiar move from Marxian *Ideologiekritik*: 'effective norms of right and justice (if correctly understood in their actual social function) are largely weapons of the oppressive class' (Wood, 2004, p. 145). But again, we need not endorse that approach, though the position we defend is compatible with it. The point is simply that pre-political moral commitments such as Williams' aspiration to 'the most basic sense of freedom' cannot be assumed to be free of the bias the critique is meant to uncover.

The critical desideratum addresses a related concern. Those who press the genetic fallacy objection correctly point out that implicit normative commitments tend to do the normative work, thus making the critic's genealogical account of the ideological belief redundant. If what is wrong about belief in the legitimacy of a political order is that the order contravenes 'the most basic sense of freedom', then the fact that the order is also the cause of the belief seems irrelevant. Williams proposes a solution to this problem:

> … the references to causation should not treat the society and its members simply from outside, like a physical system, but consider the situation rather from their, possibly improved, point of view. We can introduce the following test of a belief held by a group: If they were to understand properly how they came to hold this belief, would they give it up? (2002, pp. 226–227)

That test is hypothetical, so to see whether it succeeds we need to unpack its conditional: 'If they were to understand that they came to hold this belief as a result of a violation of their basic freedom, then they would have reason to give it up', or something of that sort. Note how the critical work, here, is done by the freedom violation, not by the causal story as such. The belief turns out to be flawed just because it supports a morally unacceptable use of power. The causal story is at most a heuristic to discover this sort of freestanding moral flaw. Our alternative account, then, will concentrate on epistemic instead of moral flaws.

The evaluative desideratum serves to make good on the realist claim to the practical orientation of political theorising. It is key for realism as ideology critique to take seriously the challenge that the epistemically focused account of ideology presents for the generation of evaluative criteria for the social order in question. While this challenge cannot be addressed fully here, it is necessary to provide at least a preliminary framework.

As anticipated, Williams' residual moralism prevents his Critical Theory Principle from meeting both the realistic and the critical desideratum, and its way of meeting the evaluative desideratum turns out to be rather restrictive. A solution to those three related problems can be found with the help of recent developments in analytic philosophy of language and metaphysics, as well as of recent Frankfurt School Critical Theory. In broad outline, the solution is to retain the importance of the causal or genealogical element in the Critical Theory Principle by motivating it with epistemic rather than moral considerations. To carve out that position we make three moves. First, we change the object of the causal enquiry: we focus not on the process of belief acquisition, but on the formation of the meaning of the relevant concept. Second, we explain in epistemic terms why some beliefs are problematically resistant to rational revision, and thus ideological. Third, we unpack the connection between diagnosis and critique, in order to explain the practical reach of the latter.

Sally Haslanger's recent reformulation of the social constructionist critique of ideology provides the backbone of our version of genealogy. Haslanger draws particular attention to 'hegemonic naturalizations', that is phenomena of valuation (preference formations, judgements etc.) so internalised that they appear to be qualities of the objects concerned. Such 'hegemonic naturalizations' are part of the fabric that allows social orders to function. They are ideologies at least in this *prima facie* descriptive sense. Only a close scrutiny can bring to the fore how they shape our common ground, a structure of schemata and material resources that all too easily escapes our scrutiny. More specifically, Haslanger's account of ideological social construction focuses on the meaning of the relevant concepts, and employs an externalist semantics to show that to uncover ideological hegemony we need to look not just at speakers' ordinary understandings of concepts (the internal perspective), but also at the social factors that shaped the speakers' grasp of the concepts (the external perspective). Concepts are embedded in social practices, so their meaning 'is determined not simply by intrinsic facts about us but at least in part by facts about our environment,' so our investigation of the concepts 'will need to draw on empirical social/historical inquiry' (2012, pp. 395–396). This empirical inquiry, then, will provide a better account of how the concept works within the social practice. For there is a difference, on this approach, between the 'manifest' and the 'operative' concept, i.e. between the concept as it appears to ordinary speakers as opposed to the concept revealed by an empirical investigation into the causal history of how the concept came to play the role it plays within the relevant social practice (Haslanger, 2012, pp. 92, 370). This practically oriented perspective looks not at ideas but at what people do by saying certain things (which reflects certain schemas of social knowledge they hold) and connects criticism of ideology (traditionally focused on ideas) with genealogical approaches (usually focused on practices).

So, for instance, Haslanger shows that generic statements such as 'blacks are criminals' are used in a way that reflects a specific form of social knowledge, embedded in a web of schemata and resources in which they are true. However, such generic statements are misleading at the same time. They seem to be making a claim about the *nature* of an object/set of persons when the claim is in fact about its/their *socially and historically developed position* in the requisite social order. Haslanger (2012, pp. 468–470; see also chapters 13–16) illustrates this by considering the claim that Afro-Americans as such are (more) criminal (than other human beings) against a historical inquiry into the causes for the alleged connection between being Afro-American and being criminal (on which also see Alexander, 2010).

We draw three consequences from Haslanger's intervention. The first consequence is to divide the process of criticism of ideology into two steps. The first step concerns problematisations of the use of language in practice through a theory of pragmatics and semantics. The second step then introduces normative evaluations that guide the axiological ordering of valuations (see Haslanger, 2012, pp. 471–475). Haslanger thus offers an approach that allows us to clarify our understanding of ideology, without, however, resorting to commitments to a politics of emancipation (or any other pre-political moral commitments) at the stage of analysis. Of course, at the stage of evaluation, commitments will have to come in but can now do so in a way that makes the process transparent and shows that potentially criticism of ideology can operate as a philosophical tool that has two distinguishable components as against the view that in criticism of ideology methods and commitment are necessarily inseparable.

The second consequence is to bring so-called descriptive and pejorative understandings of ideology (see Geuss, 1981; pp. 4–21; Maynard, 2013) more closely together by broadening the view of ideology beyond questions of justification to questions of day-to-day action. Studying how language is used to make contested and in the widest sense politically/socially relevant evaluations invisible (or difficult to see) reveals that such language uses are not only relevant to the justification of the social order, but are an integral part of acting within it.

The third consequence is to consider the question of ideology from a comparative point of view: if there must be ideologies as a common ground, the issue is not about moving from false consciousness to emancipation, but about trying to achieve a high level of self-reflection on the presuppositions on which the structures of a social order thrive or fail. At any point there will likely only be a limited range of alternative bases available for generating this common ground and fabricating it will not be up to the agents concerned or the political theorist *ad libitum*. The (public understanding(s) of the) purposes of the social order in question will shape to a considerable extent the criteria for normatively evaluating the specific ideological formations of the common ground.

Haslanger refers to that sort of constructionist genealogical criticism as ameliorative conceptual analysis (2012, p. 386). The idea is that even competent users of concepts may not be fully aware of their actual meaning in the externalist sense of the term, i.e. of the role played by the concept within the way in which the society makes sense of its world. Some might try to resist that sort of project by invoking the unreconstructed appeal of intuitions about meaning and 'common sense' grasp of socially or politically relevant concepts. To counter this objection, we can deploy Stanley's (2015) theory of ideology as epistemically flawed, rational revision-resistant belief (the second move mentioned above). Consider Haslanger's example of 'Blacks are criminal'. She provides empirical evidence (the mass incarceration history, etc.) to show that there is a difference between the manifest and the operative concepts of blackness and criminality. Now, according to Stanley, those resisting Haslanger's ameliorative conceptual analysis even after being presented with the empirical evidence would be exhibiting an ideological belief in a pejorative sense of the term: 'The distinctive feature of ideological belief is that it is very difficult to rationally revise in light of counter evidence', because of its connection to social practices (2015, p. 184). Note, in fact, the affinity between this account of flawed ideological belief and Haslanger's semantic externalism: '... while I theorize with a category of ideological belief ... this does not mean that I think that being ideological is an intrinsic property of mental states' (2015, p. 186). The point here is that there are social structures that provide epistemic obstacles to rational belief revision. In other words, resistance to rational revision is the product of social and political power used to inhibit our appreciation of evidence – the ideological flaw is an epistemic flaw.[9]

Another example should help cementing that point and showing what realism as ideology critique may look like. Consider Robert Nozick's (1974) famous entitlement-based argument for the legitimacy of the minimal state (and against the legitimacy of other kinds of state). The argument relies on common sense notions of private property (including self-ownership), i.e. notions that are in the common ground. However, a genealogical investigation on the common sense concept of private property reveals that the operative concept of property differs from the manifest one. While the manifest concept is construed independently of the authority of the state, the operative one is in fact the deliberate causal product of the coercive power of past states: the political centrality of private property was introduced by ancient states to make the social world more legible and governable (to grossly simplify an argument developed in Rossi & Argenton, 2016). So while the manifest concept looks like it can be reliably used to adjudicate claims of state legitimacy, it turns out that the operative one is epistemically suspect, given the state's implication in its genesis. So Nozick's argument cannot work as intended.

The identification of that epistemic flaw, then, rests on the plausibility of the causal account of the operative concept, which allows us to meet the critical desideratum. The debunking process does not invoke any moral notions: the flaw is epistemic, and so the realistic desideratum is met. That is how the origin of specific components of an ideology matters (de-naturalisation of hegemony, identification of sources of epistemic bias); but this alone does not offer grounds for the evaluation of a social system as a whole. To meet the evaluative desideratum, we need to locate those grounds. This is a central concern for a (radical) realist approach, for the following reasons: first, realists take seriously the task of providing orientation, which requires valuations and rankings of political states of affairs. Second, given that structurally problematic conceptual practices are already operative in thick evaluative concepts such as 'politics' or 'democracy', realism as ideology critique needs to make space for a self-reflection about the purposes of the polity. In short, realism as ideology critique needs to make sure that it does not depoliticise concepts like politics or democracy through the analytical epistemology backdoor, thus failing to provide tools for radical self-critique.

Rahel Jaeggi takes on this question of generating criteria for evaluating what she calls 'ways of living' (2014). Those depend on the kind of common ground that, as Haslanger has shown, is considerably stabilised through ideologies. Jaeggi's approach incorporates the idea that the process of ideology critique does not only aim at changing the reality in question but also at changing the norms and evaluative criteria at issue. This idea is based on the following understanding of ideology critique.

First, ideology critique combines diagnostic analysis and critique. It straddles normative and non-normative forms of theorising. This combination means that 'ideology critique as analysis means to be critique, and not just a description of the status quo, and as critique to be analysis, and not just a set of norms with which the status quo is confronted' (Jaeggi, 2009, p. 280; our translation). Analysis is 'not only the precondition of critique, but itself part of the critical process' (Jaeggi, 2009, p. 270; our translation). Jaeggi's interpretation directs attention to the entangled relationship between diagnostic analysis and criticism. The necessary combination of analysis and critique is indicative of how ideology critique can overcome the tension which characterises the realist relationship to the political context: whereas the component of diagnostic analysis covers the contextually immersed ambitions to relevance, and critique covers the ambitions of realists for evaluation, only taking them together can redeem the practical ambition to guide future-oriented action.

Second, ideology critique is normative but not normativist, or moralist.[10] For ideology critique thus understood to get started, an analysis of the relevant aspects of the political context in question has to be carried out in the way which realists have stressed on the one side of the tension, i.e. by concentrating on, to mention only a few central concerns, real political institutions, motivations of agents, and structural power relations. The normative element of ideology critique is already present therein through the concern with the inner normativity of the context in question, as e.g. highlighted through the difference between ordinary (manifest) and operative meanings of concepts. The normative element does not need to be externally introduced, hence it is not a normativist understanding of criticism (Jaeggi, 2009, pp. 283–284).

Third, ideology critique combines the goal of epistemic clarification with the goal of political transformation and hence (especially if successful) is a kind of practical philosophy. The status of flawed or pejorative ideologies is peculiar in so far as they are at the same time true and false, that is they are at the same time 'adequate and inadequate, appropriate and inappropriate toward "reality"' (Jaeggi, 2009; pp. 275–277; our translation), because they are not simply a cognitive error, but an error which is caused by the phenomena of this 'reality'. The point is that the critic of ideology has to criticise the perception of a political or social reality and at the same time this reality, too (Jaeggi, 2009, p. 276). Ideology critique is hence engaged in addressing ideologies, which are always at the same time a normative, a practical and an epistemic problem.

Realism as ideology critique thus makes a virtue of upholding a tension between objectivist and subjectivist tendencies with regard to the bases of its critical purchase. According to the understanding of ideology critique presented above, it cannot lean on an external standard of truth, but has to reconstruct the perspective from within the context at issue. This process is part of societal self-understanding, which connects to Raymond Geuss' (2010b, p. 422) idea of political theory as 'a kind of experimental science (of concepts)'. For the understanding of the generation of critical purchase (or critical distance) this means that it matters how the subjects to ideology view the situation. Their views, even if they turn out to be epistemically flawed, are in part constitutive of the understanding of the situation. Any transformation of the social order must initially address the agents from within a thicket of evaluative concepts. The outcome of ideology critique cannot be predicted, as the meaning of concepts (and often much else) will change in the process.

In short, realism as ideology critique uses a contextualist, immanent perspective, without thereby losing critical purchase. It starts from views within a specific historical context, but with the intention to transform both the views and the reality. In contrast to internal understandings of criticism, the diagnostic-critical process also affects the norms, the appeal to which might have initiated the process, in so far as they are not restored but rather transformed.[11]

When focusing on the epistemic properties of ideologies, it is important to consider the agency (limitations) of those subject to the social order. Here, Jaeggi's account of criticism of ideology offers a way to incorporate these insights of analytic epistemology, semantics and pragmatics into a scheme of critical social and political theory. The understanding of ideology critique we have employed thus leads to a conception of realist political theory as a kind of practical philosophy. Its aim is to contribute to a process of transformation of social reality and its perception. In short, realism as ideology critique fuses diagnosis and critique so as to improve our grasp of the relationship between social reality and social norms.

## Concluding remarks

Realism as ideology critique emerges from the preceding discussion as locally normative, but not normativistic: it allows checking particular claims to authority or legitimising rationales against their own aspirations while opening up hermeneutic resources for challenging the norms, criteria, valuations on which these aspirations are based. It challenges the conservative bias in current liberal-realist thought and the anti-empirical tendencies of ideology critique. Realism as ideology critique in particular seeks to be an instrument for agents' understanding of their political and social order, an understanding which may include preference-formation, ideas of the good, a hierarchy of values, the parts of the order immunised from the political process. This seems a promising way to get started on generating criteria against which to evaluate the use of concepts and relations of power in a social order. The critical distance needed in order to become clear about the current order needs to be wrested from a diagnosis of the status quo in which understanding and critique are intertwined. Taken together, those elements shall afford the tools to tackle the distinctly realist problem of distinguishing between good and bad coercion.

## Notes

1. The classical view is closely related to a long-standing realist tradition in political thought (Dyson, 2005; McQueen, forthcoming; Rossi & Sleat, 2014), and it wishes to return political theory to its traditional blend of descriptive and normative elements, against the 'normativist' (Prinz, 2015b) tendencies of mainstream contemporary approaches.
2. Whether theorising without pre-political moral commitments is itself appealing is a question to do with the appeal of realism itself.
3. For comparable points see Honig & Stears, 2011.
4. This, however, does not imply that realism is exclusively a methodological stance, as the way in which political positions are supported through moralism and realism differ, and self-reflection is crucial here, as we argue below.

5. And the various exegetic extensions of it that have been recently put forward (e.g. Hall 2015, Sagar, 2014, Sleat, 2013a, ch. 5).
6. Moreover, for reasons we shall introduce in the next section, critics of ideology ought to be weary of merely descriptive conceptual analysis.
7. Many of the texts in which Williams puts forward his political realism are posthumous and unfinished; so part of what we are trying to do here is simply taking Williams' position in one of the directions it might have been taken, had he had the chance to develop it fully.
8. We refer to all mental states that support politically salient attitudes and actions as 'beliefs', but we remain neutral on the exact nature of this type of mental content (Gendler, 2008; Stanley, 2015, pp. 186–193).
9. This epistemic flaw does not necessarily connect to conservatism and status quo bias. Radicals and revolutionaries could equally resist (and have in fact resisted) rational belief revision. However, our primary concern (if only temporarily) is with instances of resistance to rational belief revision that have conservative effects, given this paper's focus on realism's potential for overcoming status quo bias. Not only are such instances of ideology currently the most pervasive, reflecting the interests of elites, they are also particularly salient for probing the critical potential of realist political theory.
10. 'Normativism' is a term of art of recent Critical Theory and Hans Sluga's Wittgenstein-inspired criticism of analytical political philosophy (Sluga, 2014, introduction and chapter 1). It is close but not entirely overlapping with the realists''moralism'.
11. This is a specificity of immanent critique (at its limit): 'In contrast to internal critique, immanent critique is not only directed against the contradiction between norm and reality (the lack of the realisation of norms in reality), but it is rather directed against the internal contradiction of reality and of the norms which constitute reality.' (Jaeggi, 2014, p. 291; our translation).

## Acknowledgements

We thank Andy Sabl, Rahul Sagar, Paul Sagar and an anonymous reviewer for their insightful comments. Enzo Rossi presented a version of this paper at the VU University Amsterdam, and some material from it at the National University of Singapore. Janosch Prinz would like to thank audiences at Universities of Amsterdam, London and South Wales for their helpful comments on earlier versions of arguments used in this paper.

## Disclosure statement

No potential conflict of interest was reported by the authors.

## References

Alexander, M. (2010). *The new Jim Crow*. New York, NY: The New Press.

Baderin, A. (2014). Two forms of realism in political theory. *European Journal of Political Theory, 13*(2), 132–153.

Dyson, R. W. (2005). *Natural law and political realism in the history of political thought*. New York, NY: Peter Lang.

Finlayson, L. (2015). With radicals like these, who needs conservatives? Doom, gloom, and realism in political theory. *European Journal of Political Theory*. doi:http://dx.doi.org/10.1177/1474885114568815

Freeden, M. (2013). *The political theory of political thinking. The anatomy of a practice*. Oxford: Oxford University Press.

Galston, W. A. (2010). Realism in political theory. *European Journal of Political Theory, 9*, 385–411.

Gendler, T. (2008). Alief and belief. *Journal of Philosophy, 105*, 634–663.

Geuss, R. (1981). *The idea of a critical theory. Habermas and the Frankfurt School*. Cambridge: Cambridge University Press.

Geuss, R. (2005). *Outside ethics*. Princeton, NJ: Princeton University Press.

Geuss, R. (2008). *Philosophy and Real Politics*. Princeton, NJ: Princeton University Press.

Geuss, R. (2010a). *Politics and the imagination*. Princeton, NJ: Princeton University Press.

Geuss, R. (2010b). Realismus, Wunschdenken, Utopie. *Deutsche Zeitschrift für Philosophie, 58*, 419–429.

Hall, E. (2015). Bernard Williams and the basic legitimation demand: A defence. *Political Studies, 63*, 466–480.

Hall, E. (2016). How to do realistic political theory (and why you might want to). *European Journal of Political Theory*. doi:http://dx.doi.org/10.1177/1474885115577820

Haslanger, S. (2012). *Resisting reality*. Oxford: Oxford University Press.

Hindess, B. (1996). *Discourses of Power. From Hobbes to Foucault.*. Oxford: Blackwell.

Honig, B., & Stears, M. (2011). The new realism: From Modus Vivendi to justice. In J. Floyd & M. Stears (Eds.), *Political philosophy versus history? Contextualism and real politics in contemporary political thought* (pp. 177–205). Cambridge: Cambridge University Press.

Honneth, A. (1993). *Critique of power reflective stages in a critical social theory*. Cambridge, MA: MIT Press.

Jaeggi, R. (2009). Was ist Ideologiekritik? [What is ideology critique?] In R. Jaeggi, & T. Wesche (Eds.), *Was ist Kritik?* (pp. 266–295). Frankfurt: Suhrkamp.

Jaeggi, R. (2014). *Kritik von Lebensformen* [Critique of ways of living]. Berlin: Suhrkamp.

Jubb, R. (2015). The real value of equality. *Journal of Politics, 77*, 679–691.

Jubb, R., & Rossi, E. (2015). Political norms and moral values. *Journal of Philosophical Research, 40*, 455–458.

Maynard, J. (2013). A map of the field of ideological analysis. *Journal of Political Ideologies, 18*, 299–327.

Little, A. (2015). Reconstituting realism: feasibility, Utopia and epistemological imperfection. *Contemporary Political Theory, 14*, 276–313.

McNay, L. (2014). *The misguided search for the political: Social weightlessness in democratic theory*. Cambridge: Polity.

McQueen, A. (forthcoming). The case for Kinship: Classical realism and political realism. In M. Sleat (Ed.), *Politics recovered*. New York, NY: Columbia University Press.

Mills, C. (2005). Ideal theory as ideology. *Hypathia, 20*, 165–184.

Nozick, R. (1974). *Anarchy, state and Utopia*. New York, NY: Basic Books.

Prinz, J. (2015a). Raymond Geuss' radicalization of realism in political theory. *Philosophy & Social Criticism, 42*, 777–796.

Prinz, J. (2015b). *Radicalizing realism in political theory* (PhD thesis). Department of Politics, University of Sheffield. Retrieved from http://etheses.whiterose.ac.uk/8367

Raekstad, P. (2015). Two contemporary approaches to political theory. *International Critical Thought, 5*, 226–240.

Rawls, J. (2005). *Political liberalism* (2nd ed.). New York, NY: Columbia University Press.

Rosen, M. (1996). *On voluntary servitude*. Cambridge: Polity.

Rossi, E. (2010). Review: Reality and imagination in political theory and practice: On Raymond Geuss's realism. *European Journal of Political Theory, 9*, 504–512.

Rossi, E. (2015). *Being realistic and demanding the impossible*. Working paper. Retrieved May 8, 2015, from https://www.academia.edu/10140242/Being_Realistic_and_Demanding_the_Impossible

Rossi, E. (2016). Facts, principles, and (real) politics. *Ethical Theory and Moral Practice, 19*, 505–520.

Rossi, E., & Argenton, C. (2016). *Libertarianism, capitalism, ideology: A reality-check*. Working paper. Retrieved October 10, 2016, from https://www.academia.edu/20364200/Libertarianism_Capitalism_Ideology_A_Reality_Check

Rossi, E., & Sleat, M. (2014). Realism in normative political theory. *Philosophy Compass, 9*, 1–13.

Sagar, P. (2014). From scepticism to liberalism? Bernard Williams, the foundations of liberalism and political realism. *Political Studies*. doi:http://dx.doi.org/10.1111/1467-9248.12173.

Schaub, J. (2012). Warum es einer von Idealtheorien unabhängigen politischen Theorie der Legitimität bedarf [On the need for a theory of legitimacy independent of ideal theory]. In C. Daase, A. Geis, & F. Nullmeier (Eds.), *Der Aufstieg der Legitimitätspolitik Rechtfertigung und Kritik politisch-ökonomischer Ordnungen* (pp. 436–451). Baden-Baden: Nomos.

Sleat, M. (2013a). *Liberal realism. A realist theory of liberal politics*. Manchester: Manchester University Press.

Sleat, M. (2013b). Coercing non-liberal persons: Considerations on a more realistic liberalism. *European Journal of Political Theory, 12*, 347–367.

Sleat, M. (2014). Legitimacy in realist thought: Between moralism and realpolitik. *Political Theory, 42*, 314–337.

Sluga, H. (2014). *Politics and the search for the common good*. Cambridge: Cambridge University Press.

Stanley, J. (2015). *How propaganda works*. Princeton, NJ: Princeton University Press.

Valentini, L. (2012). Ideal vs. non-ideal theory: A conceptual map. *Philosophy Compass, 7*, 654–664.

Williams, B. (2002). *Truth and truthfulness*. Oxford: Princeton University Press.

Williams, B. (2005). *In the beginning was the deed. Realism and moralism in political argument* (G. Hawthorn ed.). Oxford: Princeton University Press.

Wood, A. (2004). *Karl Marx* (expanded 2nd ed.). London: Taylor and Francis.

# Realist liberalism: an agenda

Andrew Sabl

**ABSTRACT**
This paper proposes a realist version of liberal theory. Realist liberalism denies that societies must (or can) rest on even a thin normative consensus; disbelieves in regulative ideals; and decouples liberal politics and social critique from neo-Kantian projects of rational justification. Drawing inspiration from the Scottish rather than the German Enlightenment, it focuses instead on institutional divisions of labor, unintended consequences, and the furtherance of human interests that are partly common and partly clashing. It analyzes a variety of institutions and practices – including the rule of law, the market, the welfare state, competitive representative and partisan democracy, toleration, and free speech – that reveal themselves in practice to serve a wide and indefinite variety of human interests. Each of these and other liberal institutions enable a particular range of human purposes. And each may be subjected to normative critique to the extent that it excludes important sectors of society from its benefits, is unfairly rigged by powerful actors, or displays systematic and excessive bias with regard to the range of interests it promotes.

## 1. Introduction

Realism can mean many things. The version considered here has an American accent, rather than the more common English one. It is not centrally concerned with foundational questions involving value pluralism and the status of historical consciousness. Its starting assumptions link political theory to the social sciences and in particular to political science: a focus on agents, their decisions, and their strategic contexts or situations; a sense of the pervasive and permanent relevance of interests, conflicts and power to politics and to political theory; respect for instrumental rationality and comfort with hypothetical imperatives; a love of ugly facts and political complexity; an awareness that a crucial part of being powerless is standing especially in need of institutional – rather than philosophical – restraints on power; and an insistence that, given that no set of political reasons will seem 'legitimate' to everyone, state action rests partly on the authority of institutions rather than the persuasiveness of arguments, and citizen politics uses pressure (strikes, boycotts, shaming and ostracism) as well as reasons (Sabl, 2011; Stears, 2010; Whelan, 2004, pp. 289–377).

Realism as so defined shares much with more familiar English versions but also differs significantly from them. First, the kind of realism considered here is not particularly 'Cambridge' or 'contextual' in either the backwards-looking sense (determined to place political claims in the context of their own times' rhetoric and language) or the forward-looking sense (regarding politics as an art of responding to particular circumstances). On the contrary, my sort of realism regards politics as, in part, a science. Human actors can, over time, develop institutions that are ever better suited to promoting their various ends, and can devise strategies ever more likely to bring about and improve those institutions.

Second, the kind of realism here discussed is not particularly committed to the much-discussed 'autonomy of the political.' It denies that political life is uniquely meaningful among human endeavors or contains mysteries that confer on its practitioners a *gravitas* unknown in other realms of life. Competitive electoral institutions, free political debate, and other familiar, modern political practices have *in common* with many other modern social institutions and practices an uncanny ability to provisionally settle or channel human conflicts without violence, and in ways that potentially serve a wide variety of interests. While many modern realists assert a deep affinity with Machiavelli, the realism envisioned here is more allied with social science than with Machiavellian political artistry. It regards such artistry as secondary to, and taking place within, social and political norms and institutions – where those are well established. The politics of *virtù* takes on a more fundamental and radical importance only during crises, in which the institutions that normally delimit all social and political choices (including political ones) are fragile or absent.

What Mantena (2012) has called a 'moderating' realism, concerned with checking political passions and avoiding catastrophe, differs sharply (as she notes) with Machiavellianism in its normative commitments. But it differs as well in how it sees the relationship between action and institutions. Politics indeed has a privileged position for specific reasons, essentially Hobbesian ones: without stable political authority, no human purpose can be durably pursued. Beyond this, however, politics is less unique than its devotees imagine. There are indeed aspects of moral and social reality that can only be grasped if one understands politics (Rossi & Sleat, 2014). But there are *also* aspects of moral and social reality that can only be grasped if one understands the market, the workings of law, and so on. Many modern social institutions embody many of the allegedly distinctive hallmarks of political life: e.g. conflict, strategy, partly common and partly antagonistic interests, assertions of public benefit and private corruption, competing rather than consensual claims of justice and injustice, institutional norms tested by crises and by attempts, whether admirable or deplorable, to renegotiate the rules of the game.

## 2. Realist liberalism

As so stated, and as actually practiced, realism is ideologically agnostic. It names an intellectual and temperamental approach to politics and society, not a normative orientation nor a political program. This article is for realists who are also liberals: partisans of individual liberty, social diversity, progress in the specific sense of an agenda of political and social reform, checks on arbitrary power, a universally substantial (not necessarily fully equal) level of social and economic opportunity, and a true rule of law that protects everyone alike.[1] Before turning to what liberalism might look like under what I take to be realist assumptions, I would stress that realism suggests a rejection of many things that are often regarded as key parts of *liberal* political theory but which are, I claim, essential to *idealism*, not to liberalism.

First, realist liberalism regards it as neither possible nor desirable to rest society or politics on a normative consensus. Complex, differentiated modern societies lack such a consensus. (So, for that matter, did 'simpler,' premodern ones, but modern political and social conditions render dissenters' voices harder to repress or ignore.) Even liberals who have given up, as most have, on the prospect of 'thick' forms of consensus on substantive or ultimate moral questions, typically claim that a thinner consensus on rules of justification and political procedure is both necessary to liberal societies and present in their own theories. But there is little empirical evidence for the notion that actual liberal democracies embody anything like even these thin forms of consensus, and plenty of theoretical reasons to doubt that they could.[2] Fortunately, liberal and democratic institutions do not require either thick or thin consensus on the level of political principle. As long as we are willing to live out lives governed by the same institutions, we need not agree on what we value about them – or even feel conscious, day-to-day attachment to them (Hardin, 1999, 2007). To the extent that liberals value diversity, experimentation, and freedom of thought, this is something to be welcomed, not lamented. That we do not require normative agreement allows us to live out diverse ethical lives (and adventurous ones, for the minority with such a taste).

Second, neither politics nor political theory requires 'regulative ideals': principles, derived from systematic philosophy, that are allegedly necessary to orient common action and to motivate social and political progress. In the real world, political or social movements certainly draw power and inspiration from various ideas, some of which appear in books. But the motivational force of those ideas has never required that they form a coherent philosophical system – can one imagine a serious social movement suddenly collapsing when faced with a 'better argument'? – and there is no reason to think that has changed. The visions that animate social change do not derive from rigorous, systematic political theory. In fact, aspirations to rigorous reasoning and comprehensive scope are rarely consistent with the passion and rhetoric than can animate change.

(Even Marxist parties and movements are coherent due to centralized discipline, not theoretical foundations; absent the former, they dissolve into sects.)

Finally, there is no particular reason to associate liberalism with the desire that government policies, or at least coercive policies, be justified – actually or, more usually, hypothetically – to all citizens (or even to a 'reasonable' majority). Liberal theorists' focus on justification is both relatively recent and almost purely academic. No party or political movement called 'liberal,' from the nineteenth century to today, has ever demonstrated, drafted bills, or signed petitions, against the fact that the policies being imposed on the members of society rested on reasons that some could reasonably reject. The call for liberty, equality, security, opportunity, and the chance to pursue ends that others need not share in no way requires, and almost always lacks, the language of justification.

## 3. The elements of realist liberalism: division of labor, human interests, unintended consequences

It might be asked how social and political change in the service of liberal ideals is possible once normative consensus and regulative ideals have been rejected. Though asking this in a sense involves begging the question, since it assumes the presumptive validity of idealist assumptions that realists should reject, the liberal tradition fortunately contains a compelling answer, traceable roughly to the Scottish Enlightenment rather than the German.

The first part of the answer involves *division of labor* in the realm of value as well as that of society. Each of the institutions of liberal societies is liberal in its own way. Institutions do not require a shared attachment to a common good so much as an evolved commonality – partly discovered, partly learned, and partly cultivated – among those whose chief purposes in life happen to lie along certain dimensions. Each liberal institution serves everyone to some extent, but each appeals more centrally or fundamentally to some than to others. Everyone needs and uses the market, for example, but only some love it, regard it as fulfilling their most important life goals. The same is true of democratic politics and of every other liberal institution.

The second part of the answer involves *human interests* and their satisfaction as the moral basis of social institutions. Institutions rest neither on an internal and universal practical reason nor on the exchange of public reasons. The good or benefit of a social institution derives from its ability to allow a wide range of interests to be successfully pursued.

The third part of the answer involves *unintended consequences*.[3] This idea is sometimes deployed very aggressively and conservatively, in the service of the idea that no deliberate policy can turn out well. Here, I mean something much more limited: in a diverse society, no action by an individual or even a fairly large social group is likely to achieve precisely its intended results. How a social institution will respond to diverse and clashing efforts and demands is difficult to predict. Some of those responses, however, may later be judged more helpful or sustainable than others. In this sense, institutional innovation – provided it is based on experience, not wishing – far from contradicting a view of society grounded in unintended consequences, embodies a logical and desirable response to such a view.

These 'Scottish' ideas are ideologically, and to some extent historically, associated with so-called classical liberal or anti-statist positions. But here, I aim to take them in a different direction. Realist liberalism involves the study of how institutions and practices contain and channel diverse individual purposes and can come to do so ever better over time. It claims that the conflicts that would otherwise be endemic to human nature can be provisionally adjudicated through institutions and practices. That the market is uniquely privileged among such institutions is a separate, and surprisingly odd, Hayekian premise that I reject.

As it developed and adapted to experience, the tradition begun by thinkers like Hume and Smith came to embody over time normative resources that are familiar to social scientists but not always to political theorists. Too often, in our determination to subject to criticism (qua affronts to autonomy) any structure that has achieved widespread de facto acceptance but cannot pass through a sieve of rational or collective justification, we ignore existing structures' achievements and their latent possibilities if reformed. To the extent that it does value those achievements and possibilities, realist liberalism may be said to embody 'another modernity': not that attributed, somewhat unfairly, to Kant or Hegel understood as purely Idealist thinkers, but that of theorists of commercial – later industrial, and still later post-industrial – society who stressed the fundamental difference between the individualism and differentiation of modern societies and the ideological repression and pervasive domination of feudal ones.

## 4. Real liberal institutions

A liberal institution – using the word in roughly the sociological sense of an established and norm-generating social practice, not the political science sense of something formalized and authoritative – is one that meets the following criteria:

(1) *It is modern,* in three senses that are both distinct and admittedly slanted (i.e. 'modern' is used here in a normative, not a temporal sense):

  (a) It is large-scale and anonymous, not centrally concerned with interactions among people personally acquainted with one another;

  (b) It operates by managing conflict and diversity rather than assuming (or seeking) ethical agreement or respecting an alleged natural order or hierarchy;

  (c) It involves steady improvement, either through experimental learning within a given society or – more commonly – through a tendency to borrow best practices from elsewhere, rather than hearkening back (except occasionally and instrumentally) to an idealized past.

The guiding analogy is technological progress, not ancestral virtue ('technological,' not 'scientific,' because the knowledge involved is simultaneously universally useful and highly differentiated: liberal social institutions are tools that work for everyone while remaining things that only specialists, and sometimes not even they, think about deeply and understand adequately). As noted below, the quasi-technological character of liberal institutions also means that neither their character nor their results can be predicted or mapped out in advance; if we knew what future technologies would be and why they would prove useful, we would already have them (Popper, 1982, p. 62f.).

(2) A real liberal institution draws its value in theory, and its continuing (sociological) legitimacy in practice, from its ability in a rough sense to *promote the interests of all members of society* (over time and ex ante: while Hume spoke of promoting 'interests,' it may be more accurate to say 'expectations' or 'opportunities'). To the extent that it fails to do so, it is *constantly and rightly open to criticism, and demands for reform, on that basis*. There is no philosophical reason for liberal institutions to be defensive or closed, nor any historical tendency for them to be so. One should note that institutions differ to the extent to which they are capable of literally promoting all society members' interests *equally*. Some institutions, e.g. the criminal law applied to personal violence (as opposed to public laws differentiating the authority of various officials), can be glossed as aspiring to do so. In the case of other institutions, e.g. the market, the gains involved are likely to be universally positive but persistently unequal: at issue are so-called 'bargaining games' in which all parties palpably gain but disagree, and struggle, on how to distribute the gains. (More on this below.)

(3) It promotes *indefinite and multiple values and purposes* rather than giving exclusive priority to any one. (This criterion draws inspiration from Hayek, [1960/2011] while sharply denying his claim that only the market can play this role.) This is the realist version of the idealist liberal's 'neutrality.' Realist liberals cannot demand that the state be neutral; for one thing, they deny the existence of the State *qua* unified entity embodying society's political identity and normative position.[4] But it is crucial that the institutions under which we live not favor systematically, and to an excessively great degree, the purposes of some members of society over others.

(4) Real liberal institutions *allow diversity and conflict up to a point*. They encourage permanent disagreement on some questions and permanent diversity of life-choices, for the sake of both individual liberty and self-development and the goods arising from contestation and

debate. But they can only work if some forms of disagreement and certain types of choices are marginalized, delegitimized, or (in extreme cases) prohibited. Rather than leaving this fact for critics of liberalism to point out, the realist liberal admits it but denies that diversity and conflict are always desirable in extreme cases.

(5) A real liberal institution *need not be produced by a deliberate plan, nor supported by an ex-post consensus regarding its purpose*. It often, though not necessarily, arises as the consequences of acts by agents who would not have favored the way the institution ends up working. Its ultimate operations and effects typically do not reflect the desired outcome of any one agent. And it persists and flourishes, under multiple and incompatible ideas of what 'flourishing' means, in spite of disagreement among its analysts and defenders regarding its foundation or justification. As a corollary, it is possible and common, though not required, that liberal institutions be counter-intuitive: that they initially seem to endanger variety of human interests that experience later shows them to promote. (A few examples appear below.)

(6) A real liberal institution tends to *conflict with other liberal institutions in real but manageable ways*. Many social phenomena are plausibly subject to more than one institution. There is, for instance, no objective or definitive way of deciding to what extent wages and hours are rightly subject to the market and to what extent rightly subject to the results of political debate and competition. Each liberal institution tends to clash with the others, with the partisans of that institution asserting its authority to decide certain issues that can plausibly be considered the province of another (or more than one). In modern, pluralistic societies, these boundaries must be, and typically can be, constantly negotiated, settled, and resettled.

## 5. Real liberal institutions: an incomplete list

Whether an institution fulfills the above criteria will always be an empirical question, and a political one. It will depend on one's assessment of how social reality stands. Realist liberalism, as an intersection of an analytic approach and a normative or ideological position, claims that a great many of the institutions familiar to us in modern societies do (or at least plausibly might) in fact fulfill them. Here is a non-exclusive list of some such. The institutions are familiar and this list itself not unique to realist liberalism. The realist liberal contribution is to reorient our understanding of these institutions' function and value, as well as our critical attitudes towards how they might be improved or reshaped.

## 5.1. The market

This is the most familiar real liberal institution. The realist perspective would favor the Hayekian defense of markets over the Smithian, desert-based, or (on some readings) Rawlsian alternatives.[5] That markets let people pursue purposes that are diverse, possibly idiosyncratic, and in many cases unpopular is a decisive argument in favor of having them (to some extent independent of whether democratic or state institutions authorize them: extra-legal petty peddling sustains despised groups, unable to take reliable shelter under law).[6] That they do so in ways that perpetuate deep intergenerational inequality and are biased in favor of monopolistic interests are decisive reasons never to be satisfied with how actual markets operate, as well as reasons to favor their being checked by other liberal institutions. These include governments, through public goods provision, progressive taxation, and regulation (e.g. to internalize externalities, preserve fair competition against monopoly power, and prevent the exploitation of unequal information); and the welfare state, which enables those who lack skills with high market value to pursue their own purposes in ways a pure market would never allow. The benign view of markets, under which diverse purposes are furthered through voluntary exchange and through constant adjustment to others' needs as displayed through market signals, is not false but partial. Real markets are also amoral, distorted by inequalities of power and knowledge, unlikely to produce the security that allows for stable life plans, and (as Hayek admitted) ill-suited to rewarding any notion of desert.

## 5.2. The rule of law

From a realist liberal perspective, one crucial, essentially Montesquieuian, aspect of the rule of law is to ensure the security without which everyone would live in constant fear and no individual project could flourish (Shklar, 1998). Beyond this, however, the realist liberal would adopt something like Lon Fuller's (1965) position on what law is and does (which closely resembles Hayek's portrayal of markets; again, isomorphism is more common than seems possible). Law, far from representing a set of rules imposed by an authority for the purpose of general management, is that which enables diverse individual purposes; a system that fails to do so is not good law. Again, while Fuller's position is sometimes adduced for libertarian or quietist purposes, the realist liberal need not and should not concede that it should be. All existing legal systems are biased, and their biases may be exposed and fought against.

## 5.3. The welfare state

The welfare state has diverse historical origins and takes diverse historical forms. Following Robert Goodin's treatment (against its likely intent), a realist liberal would bracket ideological accounts of the welfare state's 'real purpose' in favor of glossing its actual operation. All advanced societies provide certain goods like health, food, and housing to needy citizens 'because' – the explanation is really a matter of functional result, not conscious intent – the market would otherwise leave them vulnerable (Goodin, 1988). The welfare state may, tracking various ideologies, serve any manner of other values, such as equality. But it operates in every modern society even when agreement on such values is absent (as it almost always is).

## 5.4. Competitive, partisan, representative democracy

Recent American political science has rediscovered the idea that 'competition for power is the primary form of political life,' (Walzer, 2002, p. 630) or that politics is 'organized combat' (Bawn et al., 2012, p. 591; citing Hacker & Pierson, 2010; *passim*.). That it is not *actual* combat must be stressed. Given the extent and urgency of social conflicts, Przeworski (1999, pp. 44, 49) has noted, it is 'nothing short of miraculous' that advanced societies generally settle their disputes through Engels'' paper stones' (ballots) rather than violence. The urge to replace competitive, antagonistic politics with normative consensus – which has an elective, though not exact, affinity with the demand that the results of voting not be recognized as fully legitimate unless preceded by 'deliberation' under quite stringent and unlikely conditions – reflects an idealist aspiration that democracy represent common purposes. A realist liberalism both accepts as inevitable, and celebrates as giving play to a diversity of social values and opinions, a conception of democracy as a forum for the play of antagonistic demands, within a fairly minimal set of agreed institutional constraints.

But again this position, far from ruling out reform, often demands it. Because a democratic system worth the liberal name should equally serve everyone's interests and should not be permanently biased in favor of some purposes over others, recent claims to the effect (for instance) that the American polity is systematically responsive to the wealthy but relatively unresponsive to the poor are cause for serious concern and should bring a realist liberal to support political change.

## 5.5. Toleration and free speech

A great many civil liberties may be said to benefit everyone. Toleration and free speech deserve special attention as key examples of how counterintuitive certain practices are *ex ante*. It once seemed (still seemed as late as Rousseau) as if social order required a fairly high degree of religious uniformity, that severe religious disagreement necessarily endangered civil and civic cooperation. The argument is highly plausible; it just happens to be wrong. The claim that toleration prevents more conflict than it produces is empirical, not deductive. Similarly, it once seemed as if the limit of free speech was sedition. Order being good for everyone, casting aspersions on governmental authority could 'surely' not benefit anyone. The merits of policies – eventually conventions or institutions – of tolerating not only existing religions but all likely future ones (one might say 'indefinite' toleration), and of allowing some to cast aspersions on decisions that seem to others constitutive of political order, were initially discovered in a few countries, learned through the experience of life under policies that *ex ante* seemed to court anarchy, and only slowly adopted as political best practice (this is essentially David Hume's account: see Sabl, 2002, 2009). This is a general lesson about realist liberalism generally: its characteristic institutions are learned, not deduced, and others will arise in the future of which we now have no inkling. Though there is no space to argue the point here, 'public opinion' in the largest sense may be regarded in the same way.

Other liberal institutions might be named; any list will depend on an assessment, both empirical and disputed, of how social reality stands. The possibilities include universal public education; standing, professional armies; and the expert, non-partisan civil service. The basic agenda of realist liberalism involves understanding and explicating each of these institutions and the interrelationship among them. This involves a deep normative purpose as well. To the extent that a given institution does not serve all its members equally, or is systematically biased in favor of some purposes over others, it may be faulted and should be changed.

Realist liberals, then, should not make the extreme and unlikely claim that normative arguments – claims, backed by reasons, that certain institutions are better, fairer, or more just than others – have, or ought to have, no effect in politics. The more plausible but still bracing claim, mentioned above, is that society does not have, and does not need, regulative ideals: common reference points to guide public debate and articulate a final goal. Reform proposals, and the arguments that back them, are typically much more specific than that: *this* abuse needs fixing; we demand *this* policy. And they appeal to people who would never agree on the ultimate goal towards which they want society to move, and usually do not even have such a goal. Moreover, the realist liberal's reasons for reform are *partisan* reasons. While people of many persuasions live under the listed institutions and appreciate them for different reasons, realist liberals will think we have the best way of understanding them, and put forth a distinctive program for helping them achieve the purposes that liberals think they should have. But both institutional functioning and institutional reform, of some kind, are likely to take place even if specifically liberal arguments fail to triumph. No political theory should imagine itself indispensable. The fact that institutions serve a wide variety of human purposes means that they are likely to lumber on adequately (though not perfectly) well whether or not realist liberals temporarily or permanently carry the day.

## 6. Objections and clarifications

### 6.1. *The relative irrelevance of coercion*

Marc Stears' well-known review article on realism identifies it with an embrace of coercion or compulsion as politics' central means (Stears, 2007). If coercion means the deliberate attempt to achieve one's ends in ways that partly constrain others' ability to achieve theirs, the claim is true but (as I shall explain just below) less dramatic than some think. But if it means the use of force, violence or physical compulsion, the realist liberal should deny the point. While force may in a sense be politics' *ultimate* means, and fantasies of consensus that attempt to elide this fact are misguided, an exclusive or excessive focus on compulsion greatly distorts our understanding of reality. (It also threatens to turn realism, almost by definition, in a radical more than a liberal direction by stressing those aspects of social and political life that are exclusively zero-sum). That laws are ultimately backed by coercive force is true but not, when liberal institutions are widely accepted and working adequately well, among the ten or so most interesting things about them. (There is a reason that Weber's stress on coercive force arose in an age of war, imperialism, and extreme ideological strife: force is the currency when liberal institutions are *not* firmly established.) Governments are not likely to last long if coercion is their only currency – which is why all authoritarian regimes attempt to shape, and win over, public opinion. And in a well-functioning liberal order, people obey the law not because they fear being marched off to jail at the point of a gun but because not obeying incurs economic, social, or internal (moral) sanctions, exactly the same sort of sanctions that other social institutions can also grant or withdraw.

Now that classic social contract theory has yielded to the hypothetical kind, no one much admits to the Lockean/Rousseauian fantasy of imagining that life could be tolerable, much less free in any important sense, absent social and political institutions to ensure security and coordinate common activity. But an obsessive focus on the role of coercion – or, in the idealist-liberal version, the need to justify coercion to those coerced – reflects either a fantasy of autonomy that is the hypothetical social contract theorist's equivalent of the traditional contract theorist's state of nature, or an overly defensive realist reaction to such a fantasy. Once we recognize autonomy as a philosophical fairy tale, we may be forced to realize that State coercion is not among the most salient or most serious of the forces that constrain each of us to adapt our plans, deeply and all the time, to the alien desires of others. What we want always reflects substantial social influence, and what we can get always depends on what others value. A conventionalist theory that stresses the largely benign constraints of corrigible institutions represents a systematic alternative to idealism on the one hand *and* raw coercion, whether sovereign or insurgent, on the other. To the extent that state authority safeguards everyone's interests, it does so not by embodying public coercion but by deterring – through a potential power that rarely needs to be actually deployed – private coercion. To that extent, 'the state' and its possession of legitimate authority might be added to the above list of liberal institutions, provided that we do *not* idealize it on the one hand or exaggerate its dependence on force on the other.

## *6.2. Power and interests*

One useful shorthand summary of realism is that it demotes the status of ideals in general, and rationalist ideals in particular, in favor of interests or power.[7] That 'or' is an evasion that potentially conceals a huge problem. To see politics – not to mention morality – as essentially a matter of power seems dubiously liberal. To see politics and morality as matters of interest seems much more liberal but dubiously realist. ('Interest' seems a clearly realist concept when, and only when, it is hard to distinguish from power: 'class interests,' 'the national interest').

In my view, realist liberalism acknowledges both power and interests in the following characteristic way. Liberal institutions *ought* to favor everyone's interests equally, in spite of unequal social power and to a great extent in ways that render power less salient. (The rule of law means that the same law binds the privileged and the despised; democracy gives a paper stone of equal weight to each citizen; the benefits of the welfare state are available to all but in practice benefit the most vulnerable disproportionately by supplementing what would otherwise be their vastly inferior bargaining power.) And the operation of liberal institutions ought to serve indefinite ends rather than favoring existing hierarchies. In practice, realist liberals realize, this will never work perfectly, due precisely to power. Powerful actors always try, with some success, to use their power to stack the system in favor of their own interests and in ways that deliberately serve their own purposes more than others'. Correcting this requires, on a liberal realist view, *countervailing* power – in economics (as in Galbraith, [1952], who coined that phrase to mean the role of actors like trade unions and government in curbing the power of corporations), but also in politics (political opposition, both electoral and social movement-based) and other realms.

Realist liberalism thus adopts and generalizes to realms outside formal politics the constitutionalist doctrine that checks and balances are instrumentally necessary to liberty. To acknowledge the need for countervailing power is to accept that liberal institutions will never work as purely as modeled. It will not even be the case that the problems of liberal institutions can be completely solved by having each one constrain and check the others, or having each one adapt to respond to others' failures. Such mechanisms will never work perfectly.

The question is whether distortions caused by power are so pervasive and intractable that aspiring to institutions that serve everyone's interests obscures more than it illuminates. (In the practical realm this cashes out as: whether it makes sense to try to reform institutions distorted by social power or whether one should aim to abolish social power – keeping in mind that advocates of such abolition typically lack specific and practical blueprints for effecting it.) One's answer to that question will reflect an ideological, 'pre-theoretical' judgment and one that mostly tracks, though it cannot settle, the difference between liberals and radicals. But this formulation does explain how realist liberals can acknowledge power, and even relish many instances in which power is used to check power, while considering interest the more fundamental category. Farming requires ceaselessly fighting off pests and weeds. But its purpose, what motivates it and gives it value, is not the pesticides and the herbicides but healthy growth.

### 6.3. Which interests realist liberalism does not further (and how)

Realist liberalism believes that social institutions should equally serve indefinite projects. We can, realistically, aspire to institutions that do not predictably serve only certain nameable projects to the exclusion of others. (Consider what may happen in fifty years. When it comes to the market: which products will people buy? When it comes to the competitive politics of open societies: which demands that are unknown, or marginal, now will be central then? If we do not know, that is a sign that liberal institutions work tolerably well. In a rough, though scary, sense, the less we can predict, the better they are working.) But as both defenders and critics of liberalism have often noted, liberalism cannot accommodate all interests or purposes. It will, and must, marginalize the purposes of those who would like to lead the kind of lives that require – or rather would require, if their partisans were to prevail – suppressing others' purposes.

That said, such marginalization rarely requires coercive bans or direct state action. The aspirations of the likes of Nazis, communists, or serious, violent jihadists are, in the normal case, easily frustrated through the exercise of political, legal, economic, and cultural rights by the many whose interests would be radically endangered were such sects to triumph.[8] A political and social system that more or less furthers everyone's interests will marginalize Nazis in much the same way as it marginalizes proponents of Henry George's 'single tax' – and without any more need to mount a crusade, i.e. a conscious, anxious, society-wide opinion, against the former any more than against the latter. Where this is not the case, e.g. where liberalism is new and/or fragile, state power may have to adopt a more militant perspective – but always as a second-best, and necessarily for a limited time. Liberal institutions in a constant state of militancy could hardly remain liberal.

### 6.4. Causal explanation and social critique

The above account contains an apparent tension between two ways of looking at the world. From an *explanatory* perspective, institutions can be explained as arising largely by accident and persisting because they fulfill the needs of a great many parties in society. Thus, Hume wrote that while the rule of law was probably invented in small republics, it was adopted by other societies and was hard to dislodge – a 'hardy plant' – once generally practiced, because it was so obviously useful for promoting human interests (Hume, 1742/1987, p. 124; McArthur, 2007). The realist liberal thinks other social and political institutions work much the same way, and that the ordinary people who benefit from them need no more have a conscious normative theory of those institutions than they need to be experts on jurisprudence or philosophy of law in order to benefit from, and take for granted, the security and predictability allowed by the rule of law (where it exists). From a *normative* perspective, liberals recommend reforms so that institutions, which typically benefit everyone to some small degree, benefit more people more substantially and with less persistent bias.

As that formulation suggests, one response to the apparent tension is to stress a fact known to scholars of bargaining games but persistently difficult to take into our moral psychology: an outcome or institutions can benefit all parties *greatly* but still *unequally*.[9] Radicals stress that social institutions benefit one group or class of persons much more than others. Conservatives of a Hobbesian stripe counter that they are, for everyone, much better than nothing. Realist liberals happily admit both points simultaneously as a reason simultaneously to appreciate the institution in question and to reform it. In fact, arguments for social reform very often proceed in something like this way, rather than requiring a consensus on theories of equality or social justice. A good that is widely enjoyed and taken for granted by advantaged groups is said, at some point, to have become a necessity for decent living in society, such that there is no excuse for not extending its advantages to the members of less-advantaged groups. As noted above, essentially technological discoveries could hardly work in any other way: their worth is known through experience, not deduction.

### 6.5. Realist liberalism and democratic theory

Some might object that realist liberalism is not as new as here claimed. After all, much of what goes by the name of *democratic* theory, especially in the rational choice tradition, explains and defends social institutions as ways of furthering human interests (Knight & Johnson, 2011; Pettit, 2000). There is no point making enemies out of friends. Any work that provides insight into human interests and institutions is worthwhile, and to some extent realist liberalism might serve as a rallying point for existing scholars, by whatever name, who have liberal commitments but reject ideal-theory methods. However, consciously approaching institutional analysis and critique from a realist-liberal perspective sharpens certain issues and avoids certain pitfalls. Here, I can only sketch three points, in admitted need of further elaboration and defense.

First: embracing realism, explicitly and without apology, will help us reject the idea that institutions – especially Democracy – should be studied and advocated in ideal form. For instance, even Knight and Johnson's work, which displays a welcome (and self-styled) realism regarding how existing social institutions *other* than democracy originated and currently operate, presents a highly idealized form of how democracy should or must exist as the method for reforming those institutions. Democracy, alone among actual and potential social institutions, is granted immunity from skeptical questions. In particular, Knight and Johnson's theory, like most democratic theory, shares idealist liberal theory's reluctance to grapple with the central and inescapable role of mass organizations – political parties, ideologies, and social groups – in shaping and channeling citizens' preferences and opinions in mass polities. The case for 'argument' and 'voting' is presented as if both might, without the need for great imagination, take place without partisan cues, ideological blinders, and group loyalties.[10] This might be called second-order bias: other institutions are judged in the state of their actual existence, but 'democracy,' posited as the necessary method for reforming all institutions (including itself) is judged as if it alone were likely to be undistorted by power and able to transcend non-rational allegiances. This bias is difficult to escape in any theory that still aspires to put forth ideal types as the first step in a project of reform. To the extent that it does this, democratic theory remains idealist rather than realist.

Second, realist liberalism, more than other theoretical approaches, is able to give due respect to ordinary human interests. In common with ideal theory – to which they remain in many ways quite attached – even many democratic theorists who assert affinities to (reformist) liberalism and to rational-choice models of politics often deny that the satisfaction of interests as such has even *prima facie* normative weight. Only those interests count that could be defended in public argument as considerations that others should recognize. Allegedly special or partial interests are to count for nothing (Pettit, 2000, p. 108), and 'the democratic process is designed to let the requirements of reason' – an impeccably idealist phrase – 'materialize and impose themselves' (Pettit, 1997, p. 201).[11] Deriving and justifying institutions with reference to plain-old *interests* seems a realist specialty. Insistence on doing so requires a more open break with ideal-liberal theory than existing democratic theorists can typically tolerate. From a realist perspective this break is worth risking, since real agents will support social institutions, and demonstrably benefit from them, only if those institutions further those agents' actual interests rather than those that a political theorist thinks they ought to recognize (but don't).

Finally, to study institutions and interests in the context of a liberal rather than a consciously democratic theory helps avoid a pervasive democratic-theory bias in favor of those institutions – really a single institution, the democratic state – that allegedly make it possible for public policy to be the product of *conscious* and *collective* decision. It is no criticism of democratic theorists that they are most devoted to their own topic of study: democracy, not the other institutions that shape our cooperative and conflictual lives. Yet this devotion may pervasively obscure not only the limits of actually-existing (and actually achievable) democratic decision-making but the extent to which many human institutions only work properly to enable our diverse choices to the extent that no one tries to fully understand or master them. Democratic theorists often respond by saying either that a decision to leave certain matters to private choice can and must be made democratically, or that private and social institutions themselves contribute to democratic quality. While this latitudinarianism is admirable, it only replicates the central bias in favor of democracy. It may in fact be in many individuals' interest to be able to deny the authority of centralized decision-making in the first place; and there is no particular reason to think that non-political institutions must be defensible *qua* contributors to democratic politics rather than the reverse sometimes being the case.

## 7. Conclusion

The title of this article has promised an agenda, a blueprint for a new direction in realist theory on the one hand and liberal theory on the other. Its substance might seem to lack such an agenda. I have discussed how a realist liberalism might view the world, but what is it *for?* What is its urgent normative purpose? The question is natural but so are two responses. First, there should be no shame, for scholars and intellectuals, in acknowledging that one's main purpose is, frankly, intellectual: that of understanding difficult and counterintuitive political phenomena whose nature and significance is not evident to common sense.

Second, while real liberalism rules out some purposes, the demand that it articulate its own uniform purpose, its own utopia, is unnecessary, and, in fact, illiberal. It is unnecessary, because politics and society never have, and do not require, regulative ideals supplied by theory or philosophy. It is illiberal because the point should surely be not to prospect for El Dorados of common purpose but to allow a blinding variety of diverse individuals to live *by their own lights* provided that they acquiesce in institutions that constrain them not to cross (too much, or too intractably) the purposes of others. Realist liberalism is the kind of liberalism that, perhaps surprisingly, most shares the ethos of the modern novel: its astonishment at the extent of our incommunicable subjectivity, its conviction that each psyche contains is a 'little civilization' (McEwan, 2001, pp. 35–36; Robinson, 2005, p. 233). But we differ even more (and ever more) profoundly as a result of social and political development. The further we are from violent anarchy, the less we resemble one another in our zeal for mere survival. My aspirations will not excite you; my vision for society will not motivate you; the justifications that convince me will not convince you.

Realist liberalism means constantly trying to make sure that ever fewer people get left out or trod under either by unconstrained private actors or by the institutions and practices that shape their choices and possibilities. Beyond that, it aspires to let people live *their own lives* – not the ones, however admirable to us theorists, that we would design for them.

## Notes

1. This list is inspired by many works by Michael Freeden, especially Freeden, 2005, Introduction and Chapter 1. I would follow Freeden in characterizing recent neo-Kantian 'liberalism' as a detour and distraction from the larger liberal tradition.
2. For an excellent discussion, with extensive citations, see Sleat (2013).
3. For the different connotations of unintended consequences in Anglo-American thought (benign) and German thought (tragic, angst-inducing) see Müller, 2011, p. 30f. Realist and idealist liberalism largely replicate this difference.
4. 'State' as a shorthand for the administrative apparatus is of course fine, but probably less clear than 'bureaucracy.'
5. That the market systematically and universally rewards the bourgeois virtues is (as Hayek notes) quite unlikely, and those values are in any case disputed. Smith's apparent defense of wealth creation as good for society but of unclear value for any of its component individuals is utterly lacking in normative persuasiveness. Early Rawls appeared to acknowledge the possibility of a Humean, mutual-advantage interpretation of the difference principle, but it is not clear that later Rawls has room for it.
6. This is proverbially true of Jews, Roma, and other groups considered outside national communities. For a more surprising application to African-Americans, see Austin (1993).
7. See, e.g. Shapiro, 1999. Power and interests are perhaps liberal and radical concepts. Conservative forms of realism might stress still other alternatives to liberal reason: authority (traditionalist conservatism), fear (Hobbesian or reactionary conservatism), or decision (Schmittian or authoritarian conservatism). I shall not pursue these possibilities here.
8. That is: liberalism must marginalize such persons' purposes or projects, but need not and should not persecute those persons themselves. Here I concur with Sleat, 2013.
9. Schelling (1960/1980) claimed that in his time even experienced arms-control negotiators found this basic fact of game theory counter-intuitive!
10. Knight & Johnson, 2011 explicitly but unconvincingly defend a choice to defend democracy in 'ideal form' (in spite of their emphasis on 'realism' and power elsewhere) on 165, 169n4, and elsewhere.
11. Because Pettit associates the furtherance of mere interests (unmodified by common deliberation) with respect for narrow, selfish, or material self-interest ('atomized concerns,' 'individual satisfaction') on the one hand and market models of politics on the other – both of which associations the realist liberal would strongly reject – respect for mere interests strikes Pettit as a recipe for domination, for exposing 'all weakly placed individuals to the naked preferences of the stronger' (Pettit 1997, pp., 9, 10, 205). Pettit rightly claims, however, that he is no outlier: contractualist and deliberative-democratic theorists overwhelmingly share his belief that the furtherance of interests alone can provide no normative reasons. For further discussion see MacGilvray, 2011, pp. 190–198.

## Acknowledgments

Earlier versions of this paper were delivered at the workshop, 'What is Realism?' at the National University of Singapore, 9–10 January 2015, as well as at MANCEPT, Manchester, England, 6–7 September 2016, and at Ohio State University's Political Theory workshop, 26 September 2016 (though time and space constraints prevented full incorporation of comments from the last two). I am grateful for comments from Ed Hall, Eric MacGilvray, Allison McQueen, Terry Nardin, Philip Pettit, Janosch Prinz, Rahul Sagar, Matt Sleat, and an anonymous reviewer.

## Disclosure statement

No potential conflict of interest was reported by the author.

## References

Austin, R. (1993). An honest living: Street vendors, municipal regulation, and the black public sphere. *Yale Law Journal, 93*, 2119–2131.

Bawn, K., Cohen, M., Karol, D., Masket, S., Noel, H., & Zaller, J. (2012). A theory of political parties: Groups, policy demands and nominations in American politics. *Perspectives on Politics, 10*, 571–597.

Freeden, M. (2005). *Liberal languages*. Princeton: Princeton University Press.

Fuller, L. L. (1965). *The morality of law*. New Haven, CT: Yale University Press.

Galbraith, J. K. (1952). *American capitalism: The concept of countervailing power*. Boston, MA: Houghton Mifflin.

Goodin, R. (1988). *Reasons for welfare*. Princeton: Princeton University Press.

Hacker, J. S., & Pierson, P. (2010). *Winner-take-all politics*. New York, NY: Simon & Schuster.

Hardin, R. (1999). *Liberalism, constitutionalism, and democracy*. Oxford: Oxford University Press.

Hardin, R. (2007). *David Hume: Moral and political theorist*. Oxford: Oxford University Press.

Hayek, F. A. (1960/2011). *The constitution of liberty*, (ed. R. Hamowy). Chicago: University of Chicago Press.

Hume, D. (1742/1987). Of the rise and progress of the arts and sciences. In *Essays moral, political and literary*, Eugene F. Miller (Ed.). Rev. Ed., pp. 111–137. Indianapolis: Liberty Fund.

Knight, J., & Johnson, J. (2011). *The priority of democracy*. Princeton, NJ: Princeton University Press.

MacGilvray, E. (2011). *The invention of market freedom*. Cambridge: Cambridge University Press.

Mantena, K. (2012). Another realism: The politics of Gandhian nonviolence. *American Political Science Review, 106*, 455–470.

McArthur, N. (2007). *David Hume's political theory: Law, commerce, and the constitution of government*. Toronto: University of Toronto Press.

McEwan, I. (2001). *Atonement*. London: Jonathan Cape.

Müller, J.-W. (2011). *Contesting democracy*. New Haven, CT: Yale University Press.

Pettit, P. (1997). *Republicanism: A theory of freedom and government*. Oxford: Oxford University Press.

Pettit, P. (2000). Democracy, electoral and contestatory. In I. Shapiro & S. Macedo (Eds.), *NOMOS 42: Designing democratic institutions* (pp. 105–144). New York, NY: New York University Press.

Popper, K. R. (1982). *The open universe: An argument for indeterminacy*. Totowa, NJ: Rowman and Littlefield.

Przeworski, A. (1999). Minimalist conception of democracy: A defense. In I. Shapiro & C. Hacker-Cordón (Eds.), *Democracy's value* (pp. 23–55). Cambridge: Cambridge University Press.

Robinson, Marilynne (2005). *Gilead*. New York, NY: Macmillan.

Rossi, E., & Sleat, M. (2014). Realism in normative political theory. *Philosophy Compass, 9*, 689–701.

Sabl, A. (2002). When bad things happen from good people: Hume's political ethics of revolution. *Polity, 35*(1), 73–92.

Sabl, A. (2009). The last artificial virtue: Hume on toleration and its lessons. *Political Theory, 37*, 511–538.

Sabl, A. (2011). History and reality: Idealist pathologies and 'Harvard School' remedies. In J. Floyd and J. Floyd (Eds.), *Political philosophy vs. history?* (pp. 151–176). Cambridge: Cambridge University Press.

Schelling, T. (1960/1980). *The strategy of conflict*. Cambridge, MA: Harvard University Press.

Shapiro, I. (1999). Enough of deliberation: Politics is about interests and power. In Stephen Macedo (Ed.), *Deliberative politics* (pp. 28–38). Oxford: Oxford University Press.

Shklar, J. N. (1998). Political theory and the rule of law. In Stanley Hoffman (Eds.), *Idem, political thought and political thinkers* (pp. 21–37). Chicago: University of Chicago Press.

Sleat, M. (2013). *Liberal realism*. Manchester: Manchester University Press.

Stears, M. (2007). Liberalism and the politics of compulsion. *British Journal of Political Science, 37*, 533–553.

Stears, M. (2010). *Demanding democracy: American radicals in search of a new politics*. Princeton: Princeton University Press.

Walzer, M. (2002). Passion and politics. *Philosophy and Social Criticism, 28*, 617–633.

Whelan, F. (2004). *Hume and Machiavelli: Political realism and liberal thought*. Lanham, MD: Lexington Books.

# Methodological moralism in political philosophy

David Estlund

**ABSTRACT**
An important strand in the school of thought known as 'political realism' is a distancing from, if not a rejection of 'political moralism,' the application of moral standards to political phenomena. This initial formulation of realism's opposition to moralism suggests several distinct theses. One is that moral thinking, as a social phenomenon, is causally subsidiary to political structure. Another is that moral convictions are mere rationalizations of preferences and interests. A third is that proper political thought takes the moral defects of humans as given. Another thesis yet would be that political standards are not 'applied ethics,' applications of moral principles applicable to individual behavior. I argue that none of these positions, even if they were correct, would raise any difficulty for the thesis that political arrangements are subject to moral standards of what is right or just.

## Introduction

Evaluative standards for political arrangements have an uneasy relation to the idea of moral standards for several reasons. For one thing, it is not clear how to delineate the boundaries of the moral. Another issue, influential lately, is that political communities need a way forward even in the face of moral disagreement. It might seem to be unresponsive to offer a moral argument as the solution. But that does not get us very far, since any evaluative standard – moral or not – will also be implicated in the kind of disagreement we find in politics. For this and other reasons we will survey, it is not easy to discern what the realist objection to the moral understanding of political normativity is meant to be. In this paper, I want to make some distinctions in order to identify several (by no means all) of the possibilities, and argue along the way that each of them faces serious difficulties. Without knowing exactly what 'moral' should be taken to mean, which I admit is a hard question for either side of the political realism debate, I adopt what might be called a 'methodological moralism.' Since my aims here are critical, I mainly adopt the stance of anti-anti-moralism in political philosophy, rather than mounting a substantive defense of the moralist position. Also, I am not suggesting that anti-moralism is the core of realism (though it may be in some authors). Realism is not a single view but a family of views which I will not try to define further here. My focus is several strands of critique of moralism in political philosophy.

There is reason to complain about the very term 'realism' in political philosophy. The connotation, surely not unintentional, is that realists are those who believe we should be realistic in political theory and practice. The opposing camp has been labeled, by the realists, (a term evidently coined by Bernard Williams) as the party of 'moralism.' *Merriam-Webster* proposes as synonyms for 'moralism,' 'prudery, nice-nellyism, prudishness, puritanism.' I have no proposal for substituting new terms, at least not a realistic one. So I will stick with 'realism' (though it will sometimes be useful to refer more specifically to 'anti-moralism') and 'political moralism.'

The following distinction might help in thinking about the vague idea of being 'realistic' in political philosophy. Consider two propositions that are not very controversial:

Proposal realism:

> Proposals for political action or change are defective if they are not informed by and sensitive to the best available assessment of the relevant facts and probabilities, however depressing they might be (but also without irrational pessimism).

Nobody could plausibly deny Proposal Realism, and I doubt that anyone ever has. (Obviously, some thinkers have been wildly more optimistic than others, but that dispute about probabilities is different.) So, if the question is whether to be realistic, we are all realists in that sense. Consider, next,

Principle idealism:

> Appropriate normative principles or standards for the evaluation of political arrangements are neither committed to nor refuted by facts about whether the standards are or will (or probably will) be met in practice.

Has anyone ever denied Principle Idealism? To deny it is to hold that normative political standards can be refuted by the mere fact that they probably will not be met. I do think many writers have said things in tension with it, perhaps conflating likelihood with ability, turning on the slippery term, 'feasibility.' But they also might often be equivocating between proposals and principles. Once the question is put explicitly in terms of principles (or standards, or requirements) I do not see how it could be denied.[1]

So basically everyone is a realist about proposals, and no one is a realist (in this sense) about principles. So if there is an interesting debate between realists and some opponents, it must lie elsewhere. A number of thinkers associated with the realist school of thought claim that it is, in some way, a mistake to evaluate political arrangements by moral standards.[2] I want to distinguish several versions of this idea, and consider to what extent they ground a case in favor of a distinctive method, 'realism,' as against 'moralism' in political philosophy.[3]

## Beyond applied ethics

One way of opposing an overly moralized approach to political standards would be to reject basing requirements of, for example, justice on what are taken to be plausible principles of individual morality.[4] It is not entirely clear what is meant by this rejection. Perhaps the question is whether there is a special ethics for certain political agents such as office-holders. Debates about 'role ethics' for lawyers, doctors, and others can be extended to the role of politicians, and maybe they are under permissions or requirements that would not apply to non-politicians. However, this question is not a central concern of realist critics of political moralism. The kinds of political philosophy they criticize, in which justice, legitimacy, authority, and so on are central and morally defined, do not suggest any distinctive position on the role-ethics question.

When we turn to such questions as political legitimacy, justice, and authority it is obscure what the target position that simply derives political standards from individual morality is meant to be. Here are some common schematic candidates for requirements of political justice: Members should have certain guaranteed basic rights and liberties (maybe equal, maybe not…); Certain goods or opportunities ought to be distributed in some certain ways; The social structure itself ought to meet certain standards. We notice right away that none of these has any clear analog in individual morality. An individual is not a society, and so is not made up of agents who might be granted or denied rights or liberties or between whom certain assets might be distributed. And not being a society, an individual cannot be required to instantiate any principles of social structure. This might seem to be a point in favor of the view that political requirements are not based on 'pre-political' moral requirements. That can look like a category mistake: political standards are of the wrong kind to have any conceivable application to individuals. The problem, though, is that there is no debate about this claim once it is interpreted in this way. There is no school of thought, no idealist or utopian outlook, that thinks there are moral requirements on individuals of the kind that are proposed as requirements of social justice. So this cannot be the locus of any significant debate.[5]

In another view that is suggested by rejecting 'pre-political' moral requirements on the political, some, in the tradition of Machiavelli, investigate how rulers ought to rule *given* the moral defects of humans. And they often suppose that this kind of 'ought' must, for this reason, itself be other than moral. It is hard to see why. Whether or not Machiavelli was reasoning morally, there is no difficulty about there being paradigmatically moral questions of this kind. So the view that questions about politics take facts about individual moral vice as given is no reason for thinking the questions about politics are something other than moral.

## The obscurity of political normativity

It would be possible to hold that there is a *sui generis* mode of practical normativity that is political but not moral. But if we survey the main things this might mean, the idea is elusive. As I have said, it is notoriously difficult to say clearly what the moral consists in, and I do not have a proposal. But if someone claims to have arguments that normative standards for appropriate politics are not moral standards, they owe us enough of an account of the nature of the moral for us to understand what it is that they mean. If, instead of proposing a distinctive normativity, political anti-moralism is meant to rest on a comprehensive normative skepticism, then the debate is one about moral epistemology, and the realists have not begun to engage the rich philosophical literature about moral skepticism and possibility of moral knowledge.[6] But, more likely, realists do not mean to rest their case on sweeping epistemological skepticism about normativity in general. For example, the view often appears to be that there is a distinctive kind of normativity in the political realm, one that is in some way 'prior' to moral normativity.[7] So maybe they mean to allow that appropriate normative political standards are moral after all. But then it remains unclear to me what they mean to be claiming – what precise kind of priority they have in mind, and I return to that question below.

The intention in the idea that politics is not subject to a morality that is 'prior to politics' might be to reject the idea that we can think soundly about the content of moral requirements about politics prior to considering politics itself. But everyone rejects that idea, more or less. It is an epistemological issue, and it seems to me a fairly simple one. It is preposterous to hold that one could attain strong epistemic justification for moral views at all, including for those that would bear on politics, entirely before considering what they would imply in political contexts. That kind of 'ethics first' approach is not a serious contender in moral or political philosophy, and I take it that political realists who reject the priority of morality to politics mean to reject moralism in political thought in some deeper way than this.[8]

Some who oppose moralism about politics do have a beef of one kind or another with moral thought itself. Certainly, philosophers have long debated whether moral thought can ever gain significant epistemological warrant or authority. Notoriously, moral views vary widely across history and culture. In addition, there are no instruments to detect the moral facts in the way that are sometimes available for scientific facts. And so on. And, of course, this might all open the door to rationalization. What is often not properly appreciated, however, is that similar challenges face normativity of every kind, not just moral normativity. There are no instruments to detect the true principles of rational prudence (dear to many realists' hearts) or logical inference either, or any other normative standard. Granted, there is less cultural and historical disagreement about some of these than about morality. But consider the political realist position. Either it eschews normative standards for the evaluation of politics altogether (in which case, we need this explained), or it accepts some (ostensibly pre- or non-moral) kind of distinctively political normativity.[9] But it is difficult to see how anyone's view of the substance of those alternative standards could dodge the slings and arrows that are cast toward moral normativity: after all, whatever kind of normativity this is supposed to be, there is surely pervasive disagreement about its content, no instruments to detect it, psychological tendencies to rationalize, and all the rest.

## Political moralism as window dressing

One familiar ground for suspicion about moral views generally is the observation, difficult to deny, that they often arise in a self-serving way, as a kind of wishful thinking.[10] If I like having the money-filled wallet that I found on the street, it will calm my mind if I also judge that I am morally permitted to keep it – say, on the exalted principle of 'finders keepers.' It is natural to be suspicious, or at least critically alert, when a person's moral principles happen to endorse things that would be favorable to her. This is a mechanism – leaving its details aside here – that operates at the level of individual psychology. (We will turn shortly to more social-structural versions of the idea.) Of course, some of the self-serving moral views that are so-formed might be about political matters. For example, if I like the tax benefit I get when I inherit a lot of money from my wealthy family (a hypothetical example), then it will calm my mind if I also believe that there is a moral justification for such a tax break. And it isn't just a matter of what I might think, but also about what I might want to say or do publicly. If I want to politically promote such a tax policy, it will calm my mind if I understand myself as arguing honestly rather than selfishly feigning that moral view – that is, rather than lying.

E. H. Carr, a classic political realist, writes,

> 'Ethical notions,' as Mr. Bertrand Russell has remarked, 'are very seldom a cause, but almost always an effect, a means of claiming universal legislative authority for our own preferences, not, as we fondly imagine, the actual ground of those preferences.' This is by far the most formidable attack which utopianism has to face; for here the very foundations of its belief are undermined by the realist critique.

This grounds a kind of political realism in the general thesis that 'ethical notions' are always rationalizations of preferences. This is not quite moral nihilism, the view that nothing is right or wrong. The claim, so far, is only that humans will tend to form moral judgments that would justify or advance their preferences and interests. That is an empirical psychological claim, not a moral or philosophical one. In fact, Russell, whom Carr is quoting, was no nihilist, but a kind of utilitarian.[11]

Incidentally, nihilism would also appear as nonsense to all those (everyone?) whose moral views are formed to calm their minds. If they believed nothing were right or wrong, there would be no question of justification to trouble them or calm them. The psychological thesis that moral views are rationalizations seems forced to admit that people are not nihilists. And unless such theorists exempt themselves from their sweeping psychological claim, they are not nihilists either, or at least not in their heart of hearts. The view is an awkward one, though not logically incoherent: some things really are right or wrong, though people's judgments about these matters are nothing but rationalizations of their (and our) own preferences.

A more important point for my purposes is this: the claim that someone's moral views or arguments are psychologically explained by trying to rationalize preferences is no argument at all against the resulting moral positions. Beliefs and arguments cannot be refuted by identifying their cause or even their motive – that commits the so-called 'genetic fallacy.' And, pertinently, Carr's claim that moral views are caused by (and perhaps in an effort to rationalize) political structure (or, in Marx, by economic modes, to be discussed below) merely purports to identify their cause and motive. So, it is no argument at all against them. For this reason, the thesis of morality as rationalization is perfectly compatible with the 'moralist' (or, in Carr, 'utopian') view that political arrangements are subject to moral standards.

## Mere superstructure

Carr endorsed Russell's thesis of individual psychological rationalization (mentioned above), but he also held that moral thought was, or was closely bound up with, a kind of superstructure, in a Marxian sense, resting on a more fundamental explanatory 'base' consisting in social and political structures. Marx, of course, thought that even political structures were superstructural relative to the more fundamental explanatory level of the succession through history of what he called modes of production, and also that not just moral thought but thought or ideas generally were superstructural in this way.[12] Nevertheless, Carr's general idea of base/superstructure is similar to, and clearly drawn from, Marx's.

Russell, or Carr, or Marx, could add to the causal explanatory theory a metaethical claim that there is nothing to morality except these causally situated phenomena – no such thing as true or sound moral views. They could embrace *moral nihilism*, so understood. Or they might embrace some kind of metaethical expressivism or other non-cognitivism, where moral judgments do not answer to attitude-independent moral facts.[13] But the important point here is that the diagnostic causal claims (rationalization and superstructure), which are disputable in themselves, would in any case be no support for such metaethical views. Like Russell, who accepted a form of utilitarianism, Carr or Marx could consistently hold moral views of their own (presumably they all thought that rape is wrong), or at least take the general position that some moral views are sound or true even if is difficult to get things right in the face of these social and psychological causal forces. A causal diagnosis of moral thought either at the individual (as I have said before) or the social level, however sweeping and plausible, simply does not engage any moral question, nor does it engage, much less damage, the view that political arrangements are properly subject to moral standards. It commits a genetic fallacy. Analogously, we know that arguments in criminal court are overwhelmingly self-serving, and often produced for that reason. This should alert us, but it does not somehow sidestep the pressing issue of whether the defendant's arguments can be answered. So, even if moralized views of political justice tend to be produced or even motivated by their functionality for the status quo or the ruling class (which is not to be easily conceded), the question remains in full force: can the arguments for those views be answered? (Often, prudence fuels ingenuity, after all, as criminal defense attorneys can attest.) If the arguments are sound, then the arrangements are indeed justified, though all agree it is not easy to find those arguments.

## The alleged primacy of disagreement

Whether sincerely or cynically, political actors advance and defend competing accounts of matters such as distributive justice, individual rights, and obligations to obey the law. These are often matters of undeniable importance and they are manifestly concerned with political questions, such as the authority of the state and its limits, and the justification of the social economic order. Presumably, and as participants will normally assume, some of these contending positions are right and some are wrong, and careful investigation of them is, at least to a great extent, a philosophical task. This point casts some doubt on one of recent realism's most central claims, what I will call the alleged *primacy of disagreement*. On this view 'the political' is not directly about distributive justice, or human rights, or the extent of a duty to obey the law, and so on. Those are said to be questions in moral philosophy and not political philosophy because these are not genuinely political questions.[14] Genuinely political questions arise from taking seriously the need to find a way forward in the face of fundamental disagreement about that first category of things: justice, rights, etc. There are several claims here all of which seem to me indefensible.

One possible claim in this vicinity is that the supposedly genuine topic of political philosophy – how to get on in the face of disagreement – is not a moral inquiry.[15] This claim against moralism continues to be the object of my criticism throughout this paper, but here we should consider two others. The first claim is that theories of justice and right, etc., are not really political philosophy. Call this the *definitional claim*. The second claim, call it the *primacy claim*, is that inquiry into how it would be appropriate to deal with the facts of disagreement is, in some sense, the primary or more fundamental question for political philosophy or theory.

Consider the definitional claim, that questions about justice, rights, and political obligation are not topics for political philosophy, but only for moral philosophy. One might think it would be a decent refutation to point out that this would seem to disqualify Rawls's *A Theory of Justice* from counting as political philosophy, but that implication is typically embraced. Rawls, at least in the part of his work concerned with justice rather than legitimacy, is often at the top of a list of, especially, liberal and democratic philosophers who are held to be doing moral but not political philosophy. This definitional claim might be argued for in either of two ways: The first is that political philosophy is best understood as having no overlap with moral philosophy, and since the targeted theories of justice, rights, obligations, and so on are conducted in the mode of moral reasoning about these questions, they do not count as political philosophy. The premise that if some philosophy proceeds by way, in part, of moral reasoning then it is not political philosophy is surprising and undefended. I'm reminded of a childhood friend who insisted, one afternoon, that it was not raining, it was drizzling. Surely the relevant opponent to this realist position holds that moral philosophy and political philosophy overlap.

Realists who emphasize contestation and disagreement as the defining features of the political might be conflating 'politics' and 'the political.' 'Politics' plausibly connotes procedures of argumentation, office-seeking, campaigning, jockeying, advantage-seeking, and so on, that characterize the operations of various political systems.[16] But 'the political' quite obviously covers other matters. For example, consider the question whether or under what conditions there would be a broad moral obligation to obey the law. The answer may make some reference to political conflict and competition, or it may not. The question is not essentially about those things. It is a moral question, but it would be obtuse to deny that it belongs to political philosophy, its being traditionally regarded as one of the founding questions of the field. If it is said that it is 'not a political question,' this is potentially misleading. It is indeed not, usually, a matter of practical political dispute. Political obligation only occasionally arises as a political question in that narrow sense. That leaves standing the obvious fact that it is a philosophical question about the political domain. Questions about how political disagreement can be rightly or legitimately dealt with are certainly *also* part of political philosophy, but they are not, on any plausible definition of political philosophy, the only genuine political philosophy. Of course, even if that exclusionary definition were accepted, this would tell us nothing against philosophy of the political in the moral mode. In any case, my argument here is that the definitional claim is implausible and unsupported, whatever importance it might or might not have if it were sound.

Next, consider the primacy claim, that the problem of disagreement among advocates of conflicting moral and other views is somehow primary or more fundamental to political philosophy than questions such as justice, obligation, and rights. A more modest, indeed obvious claim would be that the problem of disagreement is among the major topics of political philosophy. The point of this observation might be to argue in addition that these questions are neglected. Still, none of this would support any objection to the other kinds of political philosophy.

The less modest claim is that the problem of disagreement is in some sense primary or fundamental as compared with other questions such as justice and rights. It is important not to confuse the claim that some peace and order in the face of disagreement is a precondition for the pursuit of other values, with a claim about the primacy, in the domain of political questions, of the problem of disagreement. It is also a precondition of the pursuit of, say, scientific truth or progress that enough inquirers enjoy enough time, support, health, and education to pursue scientific truth. As in the political case, that is a kind of primacy (if we can call it that) of a certain state of affairs over certain other states of affairs (and this is all Williams seems to assert with his now famous phrase, 'the first political question').[17] But questions about those social preconditions are not thereby shown to be fundamental scientific questions enjoying some kind of primacy or centrality in the domain of scientific inquiry, which they patently are not.

Indeed, there is an obvious kind of primacy that goes the other way. Political disagreements are, among other things, conflicts in political views, the contending views being logically prior to the disagreement. Rossi and Sleat's own sympathetic account of political realism insists that, 'We need politics in part precisely because of the ubiquity of moral disagreements *about what we collectively should do, the ends to which political power should be put, and the moral principles and values that should underpin and regulate our shared political association*.'[18] The part I've italicized describes positions, sometimes philosophically elaborated, that this definitional realism does not count as political views. It is difficult to see any sound basis for this terminological proposal. It is no help to the realist to call those 'moral' views. It might be raining even if it is also drizzling.

These points fit together: (a) that there must, causally speaking, be some social stability in the face of first-order disagreement is no argument that the question of law and order is the primary question for political philosophy or theory. (b) Moreover, there is a clear kind of primacy of the first order questions over the second order one of how to go on in the face of such disagreement.

## Two forms of practice dependence

When realists say that politics is not subject to morality in any way that is 'prior to politics' they often mean prior to actual political processes and events, rather than, say, prior to political concepts or to the very idea of politics. So one view is that moral standards for politics such as standards of social justice depend on outcomes and settlements (democratic or not) that arise in real historical time out of real historical agency. On that view, the idea of evaluating political arrangements by standards that are somehow prior to or independent of the outcomes of those historical developments is nonsense. We might call this the view that politics *produces* the relevant standards. It is still a vague position in several ways. For example, it might mean that the produced standards are genuinely valid, or it might mean that there are no valid moral standards for politics at all, but only the norms that predominate or are purveyed as a matter of descriptive social fact.

On the latter, debunking reading, the question whether politically pertinent morality is 'prior to politics' is a distraction. That view is that there is no valid politically pertinent morality at all. It is a form of nihilism about such standards, (whether or not it is nihilistic about individual morality as well). It is not the view that moral standards such as justice are wrongly sought outside of serious attention to political and historical developments. It is, rather, the view that they are bogus in any case. We have considered the case of moral skepticism above, and this would be one form. I mention it here in order to distinguish it clearly from the former view I just contrasted it with, on which certain historically produced norms are valid.

This production view, if it is not meant to be debunking in that way, is arguably committed to some prior, unproduced, moral principle according to which political settlements get this moral authority (akin to the 'Euthyphro question' about how God's commands might generate morality). So it may not entirely avoid positing unproduced moral standards pertaining to politics. Still, it might satisfy some realist impulses by nevertheless letting substantive political standards themselves arise from actual historical agency. Contrast this with a rather different kind of claim that political morality is not prior to politics, namely the claim that the moral norms that apply in a political setting depends on the kind of practice that it is.[19]

On this 'practice dependence' view (or, as I will call it for reasons to be explained, the practice-relativity view), the valid moral standards for a constitutional democracy, say, might be substantively different from the valid standards for an international partnership owing to the very different kinds of practices these are. Sangiovanni has explored this view and counts Rawls as an exponent. Rawls famously denied that his principles of justice are bound to make sense for practices other than whole societies. And he later argued that, in fact, they are not the appropriate principles for the evaluation of a global practice involving multiple (or all) nations.[20] This kind of denial that the moral standards are 'prior to politics' is not the claim (a la the production view, above) that the standards are produced by actual political developments in real historical time. On this view, rather, the right standard for a given political practice is prior to and independent of what emerges or is decided out of any actual politics that take that form. The standards are not dependent on how the actual practices go. Rather they are dependent on what kind of practice is in question. For present purposes, as I have said, it might be helpful to call this the *practice-relativity* view, lest 'dependence' suggest the very different view that standards are products of historical political developments.

The practice-production and the practice-relativity versions of 'practice dependence' can agree that the standards that are relevant change when politics produces a new form of practice. But on the practice-production view it is not because it is a new form of practice, and the standards could have changed even if the practice had not, namely if the standing practice had produced certain settlements or other social facts. On the practice-relativity view, by contrast, the relevant standards in this example would change not because new standards had been produced in political practice, but because the standard that was already (prior to political-production) the appropriate one for this as yet undeveloped practice kicked in when the practice actually emerged.

To see how antithetical the practice-relativity view is to at least some prominent versions of political realism, we need only point out that it can (and in leading exponents, it does)[21] maintain that there are general standards of interpersonal fairness that are triggered when certain kinds of practices emerge. The appropriateness of those standards for those practices is not historically produced on this view, but is, let us say, 'transhistorical.' The idea that fairness is an appropriate standard for many forms of political practice should they arise is the kind of thing that many realists make it their mission to deny. Suffice it to say that Sangiovanni is explicitly developing a deep commitment of Rawlsian philosophy, so often the bête noir of political realists. I am not sure whether there is a strand of realism that coheres with that family of views and which is captured by the practice-relativity view. In any case, the more important question is whether that kind of realism would support a critique of modern liberal political philosophy of the kind realism is normally understood to propose. This appears hard to maintain.

## Minimalist moralism

A radical version of practice-relativity would be the claim that the only moral standards for the evaluation of political arrangements are concerned with whether they are good of their kind. If a political system is a monarchy then, on this view its actual arrangement might meet the standards appropriate to monarchy or it might not. If it does, there is no moral defect such as 'injustice' in those arrangements. If it is a constitutional democracy, then again it might meet or violate the applicable standards.[22] Even if moral standards of politics such as justice are always and only standards for something's being good of its kind, the form known as a 'state' might also be a relevant kind, as many have argued. If so, the practice-relativity view must be open to the possibility that there are moral standards that are triggered by the state-like form of political practice itself. For example, that view does not rule out the possibility that states are always unjust unless they are constitutional democracies. Monarchies, then, even when they are good of their monarchical kind, would always be unjust by being defective instances of the state kind. This is a practice-relative account of political standards, but it contradicts the common realist position that there are no transhistorical standards by which constitutional democracy is required or monarchy is unjust.

One could, of course, be 'minimalist' about the standards that are triggered by mere statehood. Williams can be read that way, as I will explain. But it is important to distinguish between justice and legitimacy in thinking about that issue. By 'legitimacy' I mean the moral permissibility of a law's or regime's coercive political enforcement. By 'justice' here I mean the question whether a law or political regime is morally right whether or not its enforcement is permissible. Even if there is good reason to be relatively minimalist about legitimacy (a question I won't consider), that does not preclude there also being more demanding standards of justice. To see this point in action, it will be helpful to push Williams' 'critical theory' and 'making sense' principles together and call it the 'critical sense principle.'[23] This says that a political arrangement is not legitimate unless it can be defended in terms that make sense to those who are subject to it, and the political power has not itself manufactured the conditions in which it is so acceptable. It is relatively minimal in the sense that it is clearly understood by Williams not to declare generally against monarchy or to require liberal or constitutional democracy, and so on. But it might be only a standard of legitimacy in the sense I have provided – of what it takes for the coercive enforcement of political arrangements to be morally permissible or justified. This leaves the field open for less minimal standards of substantive political or social justice, and minimalism about justice is not implied by minimalism about legitimacy. There is no contradiction in, for example, holding that the outcome of a free and fair election is, for that reason (and surely within limits) permissibly enforceable even when the outcome is itself an unjust law. That (illustrative but too-simple) standard of legitimacy is relatively minimalist, leaving unaddressed what more maximalist standards their might be for substantive political justice.

For now, focus on the question of moral legitimacy for simplicity. Here is a Williams-inspired and realism-friendly position: The critical sense principle is the only moral standard that is triggered by mere statehood.[24] Liberal democracy, for example, is not a standard for all states as such. The critical sense principle, in turn, implies that all and only political arrangements that are justifiable in a way that makes critical sense in the given historical and cultural conditions are permissibly enforceable (legitimate). Before considering which approaches this really opposes, let's first bring to bear the realist idea I discussed above that moral standards for politics are historically produced (and not just triggered). Assume for now that the critical sense principle speaks of acceptability of a proffered justification in the descriptive psychological sense: the political subjects tend to accept it. So understood, this view is quite congenial to the realist idea that purported moral standards such as those requiring liberal democracy or rejecting monarchy have no validity except as products of actual political and cultural developments – except, that is, as convictions that political subjects might actually come to adopt. They are not, in that strong sense, prior to politics.

Even so, this view crucially incorporates the critical sense principle, which has an entirely different status. It is not put forward (in my construct, or by Williams) as something that owes its own validity to its being a widespread conviction at some historical time – to its making critical sense. It is offered as having a validity that is, in that sense, trans-historical. This is not an inconsistency, of course, even if it is unacceptable to some theorists who hope to reject all trans-historical moral principles pertaining to politics. It is, rather, a kind of trans-historical minimalism: except for the critical sense principle, moral standards for political arrangements are produced by the contingent course of actual historical developments. Call this collection of precepts *Minimalist Moralism* about legitimacy.

There is a possible reading of Rawls along these very lines that resonates with some interpretations of his mature body of work. In the end, I doubt that they can be accurate for reasons that pose a deep Rawlsian challenge to such a Williams-like view, and this makes the point of more than exegetical interest. On this reading of Rawls, putting things roughly for brevity, the liberal principle of legitimacy, requiring justifications to all reasonable comprehensive points of view including many that are mistaken, is trans-historical. In the modern Western historical context a political conception must be liberal and democratic to meet that principle, but liberal democracy has no trans-historical authority of its own. Its legitimacy is historically produced in the way laid out by the (trans-historical) principle of legitimate justification. In other times, and pointedly even in other places at this time, the principle of justification can be satisfied by non-democratic and illiberal political conceptions, such as, perhaps, in some contemporary Middle-Eastern settings which lack the liberal and democratic philosophical traditions of thought and practice. I do not believe this is Rawls's view, but it has structural similarities, and so construed it would be remarkably similar to the Minimalist Moralism I provisionally attribute to Williams.

I doubt that Rawls could accept that what is just or legitimate could be wholly determined, in that way, by what most people contingently come to accept or resist without any further questions about whether their responses themselves meet certain standards (ones that go beyond requiring only that the acceptability of a justification not be manufactured). This departure may be precisely the Rawlsian move that Williams is opposing, but his position is unstable as we will see. For now, note that it seems quite possible (and anyway, it is conceivable) that a large fraction of subjects could come to share some point of view which, while freely formed (the critical theory principle is met), is morally not just flawed but heinous. Suppose many come to the view that children are available to their parents on terms much like slavery: they may be forced to work, and their education and well-being make no claims on the parents except so far as they bear on the interests of the parents themselves. This is just an example.[25]

Williams's avowedly amoral conception of the relevant kind of acceptability would seem to say that the state must find some justification for its measures that are (as a descriptive matter) acceptable to this heinous point of view – one that 'makes sense' to these people. Notice that this is a moral 'must' if I am right that the critical sense principle is a trans-historical moral principle of legitimacy. It is not simply the 'must' of pragmatic necessity. We need to distinguish between the obvious fact that obstacles are obstacles and cannot be ignored, and the much less obvious claim of Williams that the legitimacy of a political order – its permissible enforceability – is nothing but its de facto acceptability to whatever freely formed points of view are extant, however morally bad they might be.

So far, I am just developing an interpretation of Williams, or at least an interesting Williams-inspired position. Briefly, though, consider the separate question whether such a position is to be believed. It is hard to see what basis there is for holding that such execrable moral convictions among the populace have that kind of moral weight as justification defeaters. This kind of realism is a moral view in its own right, a jarring one. Even jarring views can be correct, of course, but we are given no reason to believe that this one is correct. If this objection were side-stepped by understanding the whole view as a non-moral conception of legitimacy, then it is no challenge to political moralism at all, but simply a change of subject. Political moralism is surely not committed to any particular view of what should be counted as legitimacy in some wholly non-moral sense. But that kind of dodge is not what Williams is up to. If it were, there would be no rationale for his 'critical theory principle.' After all, manufactured consent is as good as freely formed consent if the question is nothing but where the obstacles to stable state rule might be found and how they might be effectively overcome. To disqualify the kinds of acceptance that are manufactured by propaganda from counting toward legitimacy is a moral argument.

So we see a distinctively Rawlsian objection to the amoral form of the minimal acceptability requirement suggested (to me anyway) by Williams's writings. The other point to keep in mind, even if it is not a direct objection, is that whether the criterion of legitimacy is or is not adjusted in the direction of a moralized standard of 'reasonableness,' as Rawls does, recall that such minimalism in a theory of legitimacy would not commit one to similar minimalism about standards of social justice. Rawls's more moralistic approach may be necessary to avoid a serious objection, namely that otherwise there are absurd implications for what would count as morally legitimate or illegitimate states. However, whether or not that critique is persuasive the Williams-like minimalism as I have understood it here would still not be a wholesale rejection of moral standards applied to politics, or even of applicable moral standards that are prior to the products of politics. There would yet be some resonance with the realist idea of letting moral standards for politics such as putative requirements of liberal rights or democracy arise as products of social history. It is a nuanced version of some recognizably realist ideas, even if it is hardly the rejection of moral standards of social justice (or legitimacy).

## Conclusion

My concluding question then, is this: What strong reason do we have to believe that political arrangements are not appropriately evaluated by moral standards? There would be nothing very helpful in simply pointing to other, non-moral, ways of thinking about politics. Obviously there are historical questions, questions of rational choice, of prediction, causal explanation, structural analysis, cultural interpretation, and many more. If we apply only criteria in these other areas, then it is true that we will not come across the troubling gap between human societies and moral standards of justice. But that observation does not yet address whether there are also those moral questions. It is not yet the least bit responsive. If one doctor tells me I have leukemia, and I seek a second opinion, I want another opinion about whether I have leukemia, not about how acute my eye-sight is, or about how well I tend my garden. There might be good things about my health, or other aspects of my life, but they change the subject. They are irrelevant to the initial troubling diagnosis. Similarly, to 'reject' the whole moralized framework of social justice and injustice, as many authors do, is one thing. To cast any serious doubt on it is another.

## Notes

1. Nevertheless, since it might only be obvious once it is made more precise, I press the point at length in 'Utopophobia,' (2014).
2. Among many others, I count Carr, Williams, Sangiovanni. Generally, see authors (with references) discussed by Rossi and Sleat (2014).
3. Notice that this question of moralism vs. realism is entirely separate from the question whether political philosophy ought properly to investigate scenarios of full-compliance or high levels of civic or personal virtue. That question can occur perfectly well within the moralist camp, as well as in the realist camp.
4. See Rossi and Sleat, (Ibid. p. 4.) 'For realists… the point is not that morality is only weakly capable of directing politics, but that political moralism reduces political problems to matters of personal morality.'
5. There is a further challenge here for seeing standards such as social justice as moral standards, namely that it is unclear that any agent is under the requirements, but this is no part of any realist's point as far as I know. I lay out the difficulty in section 6 of, 'Prime Justice,' in *Political Utopias*, (in press).
6. A very brief guide to some recent sources is 'Moral Epistemology,' by Zimmerman (2015).
7. See Williams (2005), Sangiovanni, (2008); Rossi and Sleat, (Ibid.).
8. Even a writer such as Cohen (2008), who aligns himself with the Platonist idea of universal trans-historical standards of morality and justice, does not believe that all there is to moral epistemology is simple intuition of the standards. He writes, "… asking what we think we should do, given these or those factual circumstances, is a fruitful way of determining what our principles are; and

sometimes, moreover, responses to actual facts reveal our principles better than our responses to hypothesized facts do, because the actual facts present themselves more vividly to us, and, too, they concentrate the mind better, since they call for actual and not merely hypothetical decisions."

9. Maybe the modern idea of ethics as (in Geuss's (2005, p. 63) terms, 'the immanentist egocentric practical standpoint' – the fixation on the question 'what ought I to do?') – is deeply mistaken, or at least a very incomplete picture of the normative landscape. I await clear development of an alternative conception.
10. I was drawn to this set of issues about moralism and rationalization by Alison McQueen's instructive paper (McQueen, 2016).
11. See Pigden (2014).
12. Marx has a narrow meaning for "superstructure." "The totality of ... relations of production constitutes the economic structure of society, the real foundation, on which arises a legal and political superstructure and to which correspond definite forms of social consciousness." I use "superstructural" here to mean part of the superstructure itself, or of the "correspond[ing]" "consciousness [which] must be explained from the contradictions of material life, from the conflict existing between the social forces of production and the relations of production." My point is its explanatory subsidiarity, on the Marxian view. See Karl Marx, "Preface" to the *Contribution to the Critique of Political Economy*, 1859, any edition.
13. These are often regarded as species of moral anti-realism, but I will avoid that terminology to avoid confusion with the issue of political realism.
14. See, for example, Charles Larmore (2013, p. 295), 'Describing what ideally should be each person's due, apart from the question of legitimate coercion, remains an important part of moral philosophy. The point is that political philosophy needs to proceed differently ...'
15. Larmore rejects that view, but many realists assert it. See Larmore, (Ibid. p. 294), where he speaks of 'the moral principles to which political philosophy must appeal.'
16. Waldron (1999, p. 159) writes, plausibly, 'What is normally understood by politics is that it is an arena in which the members of some group debate and find ways of reaching decisions on various issues in spite of the fact that they disagree about the values and principles that the merits of those issues engage.'
17. '... I identify the "first" political question in Hobbesian terms as the securing of order, protection, safety, trust, and the conditions of cooperation. It is 'first' because solving it is the condition of solving, indeed posing, any others.' (Ibid. p. 3).
18. Rossi and Sleat, (2014, p. 3).
19. Sangiovanni (2008) and Rossi (2012) both suggest that this captures a strand of realist thinking.
20. Rawls says that his standards of legitimacy (and justice?) apply *at least* to constitutional democracies. He does not say clearly whether they do or do not also apply to all states as such.
21. Sangiovanni (2008) and James (2012).
22. Rawls's famous limitation of his principles of justice to constitutional democracies has suggested such a view to many interpreters, though it does not mean that he takes this view. It does leave that possibility open, although there are other parts of his view that might be relevant to the question.
23. '... the critical theory principle, [is] that the acceptance of a justification does not count if the acceptance itself is produced by the coercive power which is supposedly being justified ...' (2005, p. 6); For a legitimating account to 'make

sense' requires that it 'goes beyond the assertion of power; and we can recognize such a thing because in the light of the historical and cultural circumstances, and so forth, it [makes sense] to us as a legitimation.' (Ibid. p. 11).
24. We are forced to explore several possibilities rather than try to decide which view is Williams' own, since he has not said, as far as I know, what legitimacy is – what kind of value is achieved when the critical sense principle is met, or what kind of demand (if not a moral one) the 'basic legitimation demand' is meant to be.
25. Consider Larmore (in press) discussion of slavery in 'The Truth in Political Realism'.

## Acknowledgments

I am grateful for discussions of earlier versions of this paper at the workshop, 'What Is Realism?' at the Lee Kuan Yew School of Public Policy, National University of Singapore, January 2015, workshop on 'Realisms and Moralisms in Recent Political Philosophy,' University College, London, August 2015, and APA Eastern Division Meetings, January 2016. Thanks are due to many who were present there, but especially to Amanda Greene and Alison McQueen for long helpful conversations.

## Disclosure statement

No potential conflict of interest was reported by the author.

## References

Cohen, G. A. (2008). *Rescuing justice and equality* (p. 247). Cambridge: Harvard University Press.
Estlund, D. (2014). Utopophobia. *Philosophy & Public Affairs, 42*, 113–134.
Estlund, D. (in press). Prime justice. In: M. Vallier & M. Weber (Eds.), *Political utopias* (pp. 35–56). Cambridge: Cambridge University Press.
Geuss, R. (2005). *Outside ethics* (p. 63). Princeton: Princeton University Press.
James, A. (2012). *Fairness in practice*. New York, NY: Oxford University Press.
Larmore, C. (2013). What is political philosophy? *Journal of Moral Philosophy, 10*, 277–306.
Larmore, C. (in press). The truth in political realism. In: M. Sleat (Ed.), *Politics recovered: Essays on realist political theory*. Columbia University Press.
McQueen, A. (2016, August 30). Political realism and moral corruption. *European Journal of Political Theory*. doi: http://dx.doi.org/10.1177/1474885116664825
Pigden, C. (2014). Russell's moral philosophy. In: Edward N. Zalta (Ed.), *The Stanford encyclopedia of philosophy* (Winter 2014 ed.), https://plato.stanford.edu/archives/win2014/entries/russell-moral/
Rossi, E. (2012). Justice, legitimacy and (normative) authority for political realists. *Critical Review of Social and International Political Philosophy, 15*, 149–164.

Rossi, E., & Sleat, M. (2014). Realism in normative political theory. *Philosophy Compass, 9*, 689–701. http://dx.doi.org/10.1111/phc3.12148

Sangiovanni, A. (2008). Justice and the priority of politics to morality. *Journal of Political Philosophy, 16*, 137–164.

Waldron, J. (1999). *Law and disagreement* (p. 159). New York, NY: Oxford University Press.

Williams, B. (2005). *Realism and moralism in political theory. In the beginning was the deed.* Princeton: Princeton University Press.

Zimmerman, A. 2015. Moral epistemology. Oxford Bibliographies [online]. Retrieved from http://www.oxfordbibliographies.com/view/document/obo-9780195396577/obo-9780195396577-0208.xml

# Index

abstraction 1, 4, 11, 30–1, 34–7, 49–51, 64, 67, 70, 72–4, 81
agenda-setting 7, 12, 39, 98–116
algorithms 35
ameliorative conceptual analysis 91
American War of Independence 63, 75
Anglo-American theory 5, 31, 82, 98
anti-deontologism 65, 67–9
anti-foundationalism 16
anti-moralism 64–7, 117–18, 120
anti-transcendentalism 65, 69–71
anti-utopianism 65, 71–3
anti-vanguardism 65, 73–5
applied ethics 15, 32, 46, 49–51, 57–8, 82, 119
Archimedean Point 14
Arendt, H. 56–7
Argenton, C. 92
Aristotle 13, 17, 22
Aron, R. 33
authoritarianism 108
autonomy 4, 10, 15, 29, 40, 47, 49, 56–60, 64, 86, 99, 102, 108

balance of power 47, 66
Bardin, T. 31
bargaining games 103, 111
Basic Legitimation Demand (BLD) 84
Bell, D. 3, 39–40
Bentham, J. 13
Berlin, I. 19
bias 36–7, 39, 80–8, 92, 94, 105–7, 111–13
boundary work 32–3, 38–9, 41, 49, 55, 104, 117
Britain 48, 56
Brown, C. 31
Burke, E. 32

canons 3–4, 7, 30–4, 37, 48
capitalism 17–18

Carr, E.H. 28, 31, 33, 41, 121–2
Cartesianism 15
categorical imperative 57–8
category mistakes 83, 119
China 47
Christianity 13, 22, 28, 50–1
civil disobedience 75
civil liberties 106
civil wars 34, 36, 55
class 88, 109, 111, 123
codes of conduct 57
coercion 4, 58–9, 83–7, 92, 94, 101, 108–10, 128
Cohen, G.A. 73
coherence 14, 19, 22, 30–2, 36–8, 46, 48, 50, 67, 85, 100–1, 122
Cold War 34
Collingwood, R.G. 35
commonality 101
communism 110
competition 106, 110, 123–4
confirmation bias 36, 39
conflict/conflictuality 5, 13, 21, 29, 32, 34; and civic republicanism 64; and ideology critique 84; and methodological moralism 124–5; and new/old realism 54–5; and realist liberalism 98–9, 102–4, 106, 112
Confucius 48
consensus 5, 28, 100–1, 104, 106, 108, 111
consequentialism 51, 53, 56, 68
conservatism 33, 54, 83, 94, 111
constitutions 52, 56, 63, 72–4, 109, 127–8
constraints 2, 7, 11–12, 29, 35, 52–3; and civic republicanism 65, 67–9, 72, 74–5; and ideology critique 82–3; and realist liberalism 106, 108–9, 113
context/contextualism 31, 34–41, 48–9, 53, 55, 57; and civic republicanism 66;

# INDEX

and ideology critique 81, 83–5, 87, 92–3; and methodological moralism 129; and realist liberalism 98–9
continental philosophy 5
conviction 14, 18, 50, 53, 113, 129–30
corporations 66, 109
corruption 58, 64, 72–3, 99
critical sense principle 128–30
critical theory/critical theory principle 5, 16, 55, 81–2, 85–7, 89, 94, 128–30
critiques 5, 11, 16–18, 22, 29, 33; and ideology 80–97; and methodological moralism 118, 121, 127, 130; and new/old realism 50; and realist liberalism 110–11; and realist tradition 35, 38, 41

decline 33
definitional claim 123–5
democracy 30, 40, 55, 59, 65–6, 70–1; and civic republicanism 73–5; and ideology critique 83, 92; and methodological moralism 124–30; and realist liberalism 100–1, 105–6, 109, 111–13
deontology 47, 57, 65, 67–9
dharma 47
diagnosis 6, 35, 81–2, 89, 92–4, 122–3, 131
disagreement 123–4, 126
division of labour 101–2
doctrines 36, 39–40
domination 5, 20, 54–5, 58–9, 64–70, 74–5, 87, 102
Dworkin, R. 12

economics 14, 17, 47, 67, 100, 108–10, 122–3
egalitarianism 56, 59, 67
elites 54, 70
emergencies 52–3, 56
enactment model 20
Engels, F. 47, 106
England 63, 98–9
English Civil War 34
Enlightenment 101
environment 7
epistemology 30, 34, 40–1, 81–2, 88–9, 91–4, 120
Estlund, D. 5–6, 117–34
ethics 2–4, 7, 10–27, 34, 53, 56; applied ethics 15, 32, 46, 49–51, 57–8, 82, 119; beyond ethics 5–6, 119; and civic republicanism 64–7, 74; and ideology critique 84; and methodological moralism 120–2; and realist liberalism 100, 102

ethnology 14
Europe 17, 32, 52
evaluation 2, 4, 6, 20, 29, 36; and ideology critique 81, 84–5, 88–94; and methodological moralism 117–18, 121, 125–7, 131; and realist tradition 41
evil 56–7
expediency 51–3, 60

false consciousness 54, 85, 91
famine 50, 66, 75
fascism 40
feasibility 1–3, 7, 11–13, 20, 65, 71–3, 82–3, 118
feudalism 102
Forst, R. 75
Foucault, M. 86
foundationalism 16, 21, 98
Frankfurt School 82, 89
free speech 5, 74, 106–7
Fuller, L. 105
future research 2, 7–8, 41, 82

Galbraith, J.K. 109
Galston, W. 1–2, 12–13, 33
gateway goods 67
genealogy 19, 35, 88–91
genetic fallacy 88, 122–3
George, H. 110
Germany 47–8, 56, 101
Geuss, R. 6, 12–22, 28, 32–3, 35–6, 41, 46, 51, 65, 84, 93
Goodin, R. 105
grand narratives 31
Gunnell, J. 37

Habermas, J. 5, 75
Hall, E. 2–4, 6–7, 10–27
Harrington, J. 73
Haslanger, S. 89–92
Hayek, F.A. 102–3, 105
Hegel, W. 47, 102
hegemony 1, 89, 92
Herz, J. 52
Hiroshima bombing 56
history 1, 4, 7, 30–2, 34–8, 40–1; and ethics 14, 17–19, 21; historical realism 3; historiography 3; and ideology critique 83, 85, 90, 93; and methodological moralism 120, 122, 125–31; and new/old realism 47–8, 51–2, 54–5, 60; and realist liberalism 98, 102–3, 105
Hobbes, T. 28, 31–2, 34, 40, 84, 99, 111
human interests 101–2

# INDEX

human rights 16, 123
humanitarianism 19
Hume, D. 5, 28, 32, 34, 72, 102–3, 107, 111

ideal theory 1–3, 6, 12–13, 20, 33, 47–8; and civic republicanism 64–5, 69–71; and ideology critique 82; and methodological moralism 118–19; and realist liberalism 100–2, 106, 109, 111–12
*Ideologiekritik* 5
ideology 5, 16–18, 40, 47–8, 50, 54; and civic republicanism 71; critique 80–97; German ideology 47; ideological realism 4; and realist liberalism 100, 102, 104, 106, 108, 110, 112
immanent critique 81, 83, 93
imperialism 108
India 47
institutions 5, 12, 30, 33, 35, 47; and civic republicanism 71–5; and ideology critique 81, 84, 93; and new/old realism 49, 57; and realist liberalism 98–9, 101–13
intellectual ancestry 28, 30, 39, 41
interests 109–12
internalisation 14, 85, 89, 105
international law 47, 52, 70–1
International Relations (IR) 28, 31, 33–4, 41, 47, 52
Italy 63–4

Jaeggi, R. 92, 94
Japan 56
Johnson, J. 112
justice 6, 8, 12, 29–30, 32, 36; and civic republicanism 66–8, 70–1, 73–5; and ideology critique 82–3, 86, 88; and methodological moralism 119, 123–6, 128, 130–1; and new/old realism 46, 50, 52–3, 57–60; and realist liberalism 99, 111

Kant, I. 3–4, 13, 15, 17, 22, 32, 34, 47, 57–60, 102
Kennan, G. 41, 52
Knight, J. 112

leadership 50, 53
legal order 52, 54–6, 59–60, 67, 105
legitimacy 2, 4, 16, 19–20, 29, 36; and and ideology critique 84–8, 91–2; and civic republicanism 75; legitimating work 34, 38–9, 41; and methodological moralism 119, 124, 128–31; and new/old realism

46–7, 55–6, 59–60; and realist liberalism 98, 103, 106, 109
Lenin, V.I. 32
liberalism 2–5, 12, 15–19, 28–30, 32–3, 36; and ideology critique 81, 83–4, 87, 94; liberal ironism 16; and methodological moralism 124, 127–30; and new/old realism 47, 54–60; realist liberalism 98–116; and realist tradition 38–41
libertarianism 40, 105
liberty/liberties 5, 21, 59, 67, 70, 86, 100–1, 103, 109, 119
lived experiences 13–14, 48, 54, 57
Locke, J. 19, 36, 108

Machiavelli, N. 7, 28–9, 31–4, 40, 47, 73, 99, 119
Mackinder, H.J. 52
McQueen, A. 3, 7, 28–45
Madison, J. 32–3
Mantena, K. 32–3, 41, 99
markets 5, 99, 101, 103–6, 110
Marx, K. 47, 50, 122
Marxism 55, 88, 101, 122
Mearsheimer, J. 28
metaphysics 18, 57–8, 82, 89
Middle East 129
Mill, J.S. 19
minimalism 86, 91, 127–30
Montesquieu, Baron de 32–3, 105
moral philosophy 4–5, 10–11, 13, 15–16, 46–7, 120, 123–4
moralism 6, 12, 21, 29–30, 34–5, 50–1; and civic republicanism 64–7; and ideology critique 81–4, 87–9, 93; methodological moralism 117–34; and new/old realism 54–5, 59–60; as window dressing 121
morality 4–7, 10–27, 29, 35, 46–60, 74; and ideology critique 81–3, 86–90, 92; and methodological moralism 118–23, 125–31; and realist liberalism 99–101, 108–9, 111
Morgenthau, H. 7, 28, 31, 33, 38, 41, 52
multiculturalism 56

Nagasaki bombing 56
Nardin, T. 3–4, 31, 46–62
Nazism 47, 110
negative freedom 58
neo-Kantianism 15, 22, 32, 57–8
neo-republicanism 63–4, 70
new realism movement 46–62
Niebuhr, R. 7, 33, 41, 52

Nietzsche, F.W. 3, 13, 17–18, 21, 28, 32, 34, 50
nihilism 14–15, 121–2, 126
non-ideal theory 3, 47, 82–3
normativity 2–6, 11, 13, 15, 17, 20; and civic republicanism 63–5, 67, 72; and ethics 22; and ideology critique 81–4, 87–8, 90–4; and methodological moralism 117–18, 120–1, 126; and new/old realism 47; obscurity of 120; and realist liberalism 99–104, 106–7, 111–13; and realist tradition 29, 33, 35–6
North America 16–17, 47, 98, 106
Nozick, R. 21, 91–2
nuclear weapons 38

Oakeshott, M. 53–5
obligations 14, 50, 52, 55, 57–8, 123–4
ochlocracy 73
oligarchy 70, 73
ontology 4, 64, 84

patriotism 16
Peloponnesian War 34
Pettit, P. 5, 63–79
philosophy 1, 4–7, 10–19, 21–2, 29–30, 32–3; and civic republicanism 63–4, 66–7, 69, 71, 73–5; and ideology critique 93–4; and methodological moralism 117–34; and new/old realism 46–8, 50–1, 54, 57–8, 60; philosophy of language 5, 89–90; and realist liberalism 98, 100, 103, 108, 111, 113; and realist tradition 35–8
Plato 7, 13–14, 17, 29, 50–1
pluralism 30, 55, 86, 98, 104
political philosophy 11, 15–18, 21–2, 29–30, 32, 35–6; and civic republicanism 63–4, 67, 69, 71, 74–5; and methodological moralism 117–34; and new/old realism 47, 51; and realist tradition 38
political realism 28–46, 48–50, 57, 59–60, 125, 127; and anti-deontologism 65, 67–9; and anti-moralism 64–7; and anti-transcendentalism 65, 69–71; and anti-utopianism 65, 71–3; and anti-vanguardism 65, 73–5; and civic republicanism 63–79; definitions 29; as ideology critique 80–97; meanings of 47–50; and methodological moralism 117–34; political ethics 11; political order 29, 32, 34, 36, 40, 58–60, 82, 87–8, 107, 130; political questions 84, 86–7, 125; and politics 53–5

political science 7, 47, 98, 106
political theory 1, 4, 6, 81–4, 89, 93–4; and autonomy 56–60; case for 10–27; and ethics 10–27; and methodological moralism 118, 123; and new/old realism 46–52, 59–60; and postwar theory 7; and realist liberalism 98, 100, 102, 107; and realist tradition 28, 30–5, 41
Polybius 73
positive freedom 58
poststructuralism 48
poverty 68
power relations 17–18, 65–8, 83, 86–8, 92–4, 98, 105, 109–10
practice-dependence/practice-relativity view 125–8
pragmatics/pragmatism 3, 48, 90, 94, 130
Price, R. 75
primacy claim 123–6
Prinz, J. 4–6, 80–97
propaganda 130
prudence 35, 47–8, 50–4, 60, 120, 123
Przeworski, A. 106
psychology 14, 19, 49, 71–2, 111, 121–3, 128
Putnam, H. 48

Quine, W.V. 48

radicalism 3, 29, 31, 75, 80–1, 99, 108, 110–11, 127
Rand, A. 18
rationality 13–14, 17, 30, 53, 98, 109, 111–12, 120, 131
Rawls, J. 1, 7, 12, 17–18, 29–30, 46–7, 54–60, 65–71, 73, 81, 124, 126, 129–30
realism 1, 6; dry realism 2; and future research 7–8; as ideology critique 80–97; interpretive realism 3; and liberalism 98–116; and methodological moralism 117–34; and morality 10–27; new realism movement 46–62; new/old 46–62; programmatic realism 4; realist arguments 3; realist theory 2; realist thinkers 3; and realist tradition 28–45; realist tradition 28–45; realist turn 10; themes of 50–3; three futures of 2–5; types of 2; wet realism 2
*Realpolitik* 33, 41, 50
recovery work 33, 38–9, 41
reform 71, 100, 102–3, 106–7, 109, 111–12
relativism 15
religion 22, 106

138

# INDEX

Renaissance 63
Rengger, N. 31
representation 106
republicanism 3, 5, 29–30, 37, 59, 63–79, 111
Romans 63
Rorty, R. 16
Rossi, E. 4–6, 34, 80–97, 125
Rousseau, J.J. 64, 106, 108
rule of law 54, 60, 100, 105, 109, 111
Russell, B. 121–2

Sabl, A. 1–9, 98–116
Sagar, R. 1–9
St Augustine 6, 28, 34
St Paul 28
Sangiovanni, A. 126–7
scaffolding 4
scepticism 13–14, 17–22, 33, 35, 49–52, 64, 112, 120, 126
Scheuerman, W. 33
Schlosser, J.A. 33
Schmitt, C. 28, 32, 34, 54–5
Schwarzenberger, G. 52
science 48–9, 93, 99, 103, 120, 125–6
Scotland 101–2
Secondat, C.L. de (Montesquieu) 32–3, 105
security 3, 6, 47, 52, 67, 101, 105
sedition 107
selection bias 36–7, 39
self-reflection 81, 85, 91–2
semantics 89–91, 94
Sen, A. 66, 69, 82
Shklar, J. 18
Sidgwick, H. 7
Simmons, A.J. 70
Singapore University 1
Singer, P. 50
Skinner, Q. 35–7
slavery 59, 129
Sleat, M. 2–4, 6–7, 10–27, 32, 34, 125
Smith, A. 66, 102, 105
social construction 82, 89–92, 94
social contract 108
social media 54
social sciences 98–9, 102
socialism 29–30, 87
sociology 14, 55, 71–2, 102
Somalia 34
Sophocles 7
sovereignty 52, 64, 70, 108
Soviet Union 47
Spykman, N. 52
Stanley, J. 91

state 20, 38, 47, 49, 55–6, 58–60; and civic republicanism 67, 71, 73; and ideology critique 86, 91–2; and methodological moralism 123, 127–8, 130; and realist liberalism 103, 105–6, 108–10, 112; reasons of state 51–3, 59; welfare state 5, 105–6, 109
status quo bias 80–7, 92, 94, 123
Stears, M. 108
Strawson, P.F. 48
structural model 20
superstructure 122–3
sustainability 65, 71–3, 102

taxation 105, 110, 121
theory of right 57–8
thinking capacity 56–7
Thucydides 7, 28, 31–2, 34, 36, 50
toleration 106–7
torture 19, 59
totalitarianism 54, 56
tradition/tradition-building 3, 5, 47, 50–1, 63–4, 67; and civic republicanism 73, 75; and ideology critique 81, 90; and realist liberalism 102, 108; realist tradition 28–45
transcendentalism 65, 69–71, 81
transparency 3
truth/truthfulness 2–4, 6–7, 16–17, 19, 21–2, 34, 48, 54, 60, 88, 93, 125

unintended consequences 101–2
unions 109
United States (US) 73, 90
universalism 12, 15–16, 29, 35, 47, 51, 65, 67–8, 75, 100–1, 121
utilitarianism 13, 20, 22, 51, 53, 57, 121–2
utopianism 12, 17, 29–30, 49, 65, 71–3, 84, 113, 119, 121–2

values 14–17, 20–1, 29–31, 35, 39, 41; and civic republicanism 64–7, 74; and ideology critique 94; and methodological moralism 125–6; and new/old realism 51; and realist liberalism 98, 100–3, 105–6, 108, 110
vanguardism 65, 73–5
violence 19, 38, 54, 99, 103, 106, 108, 110, 113
virtue 48, 57–8, 64, 69, 72, 93, 99, 103

Waltz, K. 28, 41
Walzer, M. 54, 56
Weber, M. 28, 32, 34, 53, 108

welfare state 5, 105–6, 109
Wells, H.G. 40
West 17, 41, 47, 129
Western Europe 17
Wight, M. 31

Williams, B. 12–22, 28, 33, 46, 49–51, 55, 57, 59–60, 81, 84–7, 118, 126, 128–30
wishful thinking 16, 21–2, 121
Wittgenstein, L. 7, 18